LINCOLN TALES OF MYSTERY AND MURDER

Other areas covered in this series include:

Berkshire

Buckinghamshire

Cheshire

Cornwall

Derbyshire

Devon

East Anglia

Essex

Hampshire

Hertfordshire

Kent

Leicestershire and Rutland

Lincolnshire

Nottinghamshire

Somerset

Surrey

Sussex

Warwickshire

LINCOLNSHIRE TALES OF MYSTERY AND MURDER

---❀---

Adrian Gray

COUNTRYSIDE BOOKS
NEWBURY, BERKSHIRE

First published 2004
© Adrian Gray 2004

COUNTRYSIDE BOOKS
3 Catherine Road
Newbury, Berkshire

To view our complete range of books,
please visit us at
www.countrysidebooks.co.uk

ISBN 1 85306 859 4

To Lance Wingad – a dedicated 'Yellowbelly'

Designed by Mon Mohan

Produced through MRM Associates Ltd., Reading
Typeset by Mac Style Ltd, Scarborough, N. Yorkshire
Printed by J.W. Arrowsmith Ltd., Bristol

Contents

MAP OF LINCOLNSHIRE

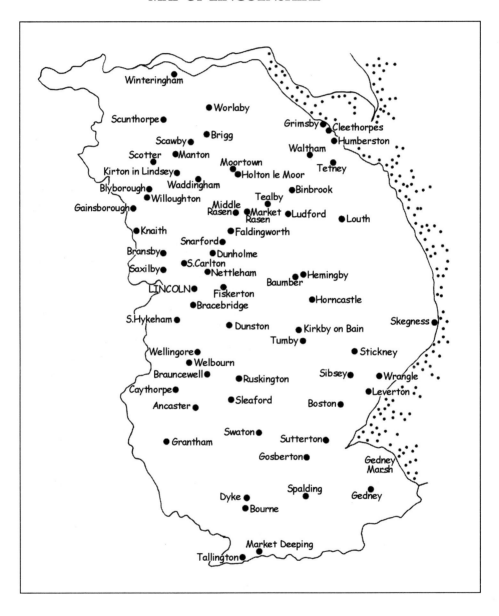

THE DREADFUL LEGEND OF
TOM OTTER

———————— ❁ ————————

To the west of Lincoln lies a large, flat damp area, which stretches out for miles until it reaches the grey waters of the Trent. This was the scene of a famous and brutal killing, and one which led to some amazing, unexplained events following the murderer's execution.

It was a forbidding area in which to find a way home. Long, featureless lanes crossed the landscape, occasionally passing over a deep dyke. Only a few small woodland plantations would have sheltered the traveller from a biting easterly wind, with few hamlets or villages to provide respite from the elements. The only village of any size for miles around was Saxilby, with its old pubs lining the Fosse Dyke canal. One can well understand that a humble workman from nearby Doddington might have wanted to stop in Saxilby for a few drinks before trudging the next three miles home.

One dark and miserable night in November 1805, John Dunkerley rather overstayed his time in good company at the pub and drank too much before taking the long walk home along dark country lanes. The prospect of being up early for work the next day, however, coupled with the realisation that the night could only get colder, eventually stirred him into action and so he said goodbye to what passed for the 'bright lights' of Saxilby.

Dunkerley staggered uncertainly over the wooden bridge across the Fosse Dyke and turned off along the country lane that

The scene of the murder by Tom Otter, still a lonely spot

led down between hedges into Lincolnshire's 'moorland'. He could see no other travellers on the road and was probably glad – for many a wanderer would not have thought twice about pushing a drunk in the dyke to rob him of whatever the publican had not taken. Maybe he would have been able to see the faint light or two from houses on the edge of Harby to the west, but otherwise Dunkerley was surrounded by complete blackness.

At the end of the long lane from Saxilby was a crossroads. To the west was Harby, north went to Drinsey Nook where there was another lonely pub for the boatmen on the Fosse Dyke, and south led to Doddington itself. But Dunkerley was overcome with tiredness and the drink had caught up with him. So he wandered off the road and into a 'stubble close' where he sank down to the ground and went straight to sleep. He was to have a rude awakening, however, and witness an atrocity which he did not confess to having seen, until his dying day.

In his later account he told of being woken by the voice of a man saying, 'Sit down, you can rest here.' The man was speaking to a young, pregnant woman. The man, Tom Otter, then sat down near to where Dunkerley was lying. Dunkerley said and did nothing, though he never really explained the reason for his silence – perhaps he thought an amorous couple had ended up by chance in this remote spot to provide him with some late-night entertainment. The mood of the couple was anything but romantic, however, and Dunkerley watched, terrified, as Otter pulled a hedge-stake out of the ground. He was impressed by the stranger's strength as he seemed to have drawn it two feet out of the soil.

Otter grasped the hedge-stake and strode across to the young woman, one Mary Kirkham. 'This will finish my knob-stick wedding,' he shouted at her, referring to what many others called a 'shotgun wedding.' He took three steps and struck her across the head. As she fell to the ground, he hit her once more. Dunkerley described the noise as like the hitting of a turnip. Perhaps Dunkerley held his silence for so many years out of shame because he could, perhaps, have saved Mary from her death, or maybe it was the fear that he too might become a victim.

Whatever the reason the murder that Dunkerley witnessed is one of the most famous in Lincolnshire history. Until the Beverley Allitt case, Tom Otter was probably the county's most notorious murderer. To this day there is even a petrol station named after him, on the A57 just west of Saxilby, as well as a lane and a bridge. Yet he was not especially notorious at the time since he was simply the perpetrator of a grubby and unspectacular crime. It was the manner of his death, however, and the legends that attached themselves afterwards that ensured his place in history.

For example, no such person as 'Tom Otter' was ever tried and executed for murder at Lincoln. He was tried under the name of Thomas Temporel, an unusual name perhaps of

French origin, but interestingly a name that did occur just across the Trent in Bothamsall in 1725.

So was Temporel his real name, or Otter? The latter seems most likely, for the surname was very common in the late 1700s in the villages of east Nottinghamshire. We can find the actual name Thomas Otter at East Markham, Rampton, Laneham and several other places in that vicinity. The *Stamford Mercury* reported that he had been born at 'Truswell', which could be the hamlet of Treswell very near to Rampton. All sources agree that Otter had a wife before he came to Lincoln, and the *Mercury* reported that both his wife and their child lived in a village near Southwell.

Tom Otter's 'profession' was a 'labouring banker'. Though this makes him sound like he spent his days checking accounts,

The Sun Inn at Saxilby where incriminating evidence against Tom Otter was uncovered at the inquest

in reality it meant that he worked on banks and dykes such as those along the Trent and the many drainage ditches between the river and Lincoln. No doubt this gave him many opportunities to stay away from home and to accumulate girlfriends. We know also that he stated his age to be 28 and he was a 'stout make' and five feet nine inches.

It seems Otter's romantic activities eventually led to a young woman becoming pregnant by him and pressure being put on him to marry her. According to contemporary reports, Otter married Mary Kirkham at South Hykeham on 3rd November 1805 and then the couple headed north-west out of the city. They stopped to drink at the Sun Inn, Saxilby, and then continued westwards. Near a crossroads between Saxilby and Harby, Otter killed his young companion, as witnessed by Dunkerley, by 'dashing her skull to pieces'. He had probably been fuming that he had been trapped into this undesirable wedding in the first place. Not only that, under the rules of the Poor Law at the time, he would have been financially liable for the support of mother and child, as well as his 'other family' somewhere in Nottinghamshire!

An inquest at the Sun Inn on 5th November ruled that 'Mary Kirkham otherwise Temporel', aged about 24, had been 'wilfully murdered' by 'Thomas Otter otherwise Temporel.' The body of the dead woman was stretched out on a table in front of a crowd. The supposed murder weapon, a hedge-stake, had been found in a field. It was produced at the inquest and put into Otter's hands.

Otter's trial took place tried at Lincoln on 12th March, before Justice Graham. It lasted five hours, but although several witnesses contributed to the case against him, all the evidence was 'wholly circumstantial'. Otter himself offered no defence and was impassive; 'neither did he change countenance at the dreadful sentence pronounced upon him,' though he did confess to a minister and the gaol keeper shortly before his execution.

Otter was hanged on 14th March, two days after the trial. His body was then taken out of Lincoln to be gibbeted at the scene of his crime. The gibbet was a type of cage, which surrounded the corpse, so that he continued to be imprisoned even after death. This was delayed until the 20th March, however, due to problems in getting irons for the gibbet made. This was eventually done by the Saxilby blacksmith, Dick Naylor. The body also had to be dipped in pitch.

But, it is the subsequent events that make the legend of Tom Otter both exciting and fanciful! Otter's body was taken out of the city in irons and the officials stopped at Saxilby. One detail to add here is that, according to legend, the swing-bridge or draw-bridge over the Fosse Dyke at Saxilby broke after the body and gibbet passed over it.

The grim procession proceeded then to the crossroads west of Saxilby where the murder had taken place. It was a very windy day, however, and raising the 30ft gibbet into position using block and tackle was very difficult. Twice it came down, once killing one of the workmen trying to erect it.

Meanwhile, the hedge-stake which had been used to carry out the murder came into the possession of George Cartwright of Thorney . He kept it for a year. It was put on display at the Sun Inn, but it disappeared on the first anniversary of the murder and was found the next morning in a field at the very spot where it had been discovered originally! The cynical observer might argue that the display of the murder weapon was a way of drumming up business. Its annual disappearance from whichever pub happened to be housing it also helped to increase takings!

It vanished from the Pee-wit pub alongside the Fosse Dyke two years in a row, so the next year the Saxilby blacksmith was asked to make some iron staples to hold it fast to the wall. What a surprise when it vanished nonetheless, again being found in its regular spot and the staples being thrown through the blacksmith's window! Even when a group of people sat up

A body might hang on a gibbet for a great many years

to midnight to watch it, the hedge-stake still disappeared. Similar problems were encountered during its stay at the Drinsey Nook pub.

Finally, according to one account, the haunted hedge stake was eventually burnt in Minster Yard at Lincoln on the orders of the bishop.

Meanwhile Otter's gibbet remained quite an attraction for local people with nothing better to do on a Sunday afternoon. It seems many came out from Lincoln to picnic beneath the rotting corpse as it swung despondently in the breeze. Eventually birds are said to have built a nest in the vacant skull, leading to a rhyme:

The living dwell within the dead
The old go out to fetch in bread
To feed the young within the head.

Although there are a number of stories about the eventual demise of the gibbet, it mostly survived until about 1850 when it fell down, whereupon pieces of it were made into souvenirs. Even today, the lane is still a remote and lonely spot which on a windswept winter's night is not a pleasant place to be. Rain drives across the flat moorland, the trees rustle their leafless arms in the dark, and the fanciful traveller can perhaps still hear a faint creaking sound as Otter's corpse moves backwards and forwards, dangling from its gibbet.

CAUTIONARY TALES

——— ❀ ———

In the 17th century there were no local newspapers to report scenes of criminal activity in obscure parts of the country. Although there are few accounts of murders committed during this period, we do know quite a lot about three murders committed in Lincolnshire during the 1600s. The publishers of religious tracts used these stories as a warning to the sinners of Lincolnshire in an effort to rescue them from the brink of eternal damnation!

The Long Arm of Justice: Holton-le-Moor c1581–1606

Thomas Cash was a young tailor who lived in the small town of Holton-le-Moor in about 1581. Cash was unhappily married to Ellen Greame. She came from a good family and presumably, therefore, brought him a worthwhile dowry. So it may well be that the marriage had been prompted more by financial gain than by love on Cash's part.

The Cash family consisted of only one child because, as the religious pamphlet states, husband and wife 'lived very unquietly together'. One of the causes of this disquiet was a neighbour, Mrs Newton.

After a few years of marriage Ellen became ill with what was termed 'lingering sickness', placing additional pressure both on her husband and their servant, Anne Pottes. She was a fitful and difficult patient, so her husband took to spending most of his time with Mrs Newton. Mrs Cash presumed that her husband 'kept' this woman and 'had the use of' her and although Cash did not admit to it, 'presumption was very great'. There was certainly plenty of opportunity to form a relationship, for the wife's illness apparently lasted seven years.

During this time Anne Pottes the servant seems to have begun harbouring some schemes of her own, perhaps dreaming of replacing both Mrs Cash and Mrs Newton in her employer's affections. She began to hint that life might be better without the invalid, and that the illness provided a wonderful opportunity for Cash to do away with his spouse altogether. In those days medical opinion was rarely sought, and the killing of a sickly woman would be an easy matter in practice if not in conscience.

And so it was that one day, when Ellen Cash was sitting by the fire, her husband killed her by smothering her with a cloth over the face. The woman was too weak to struggle and the deed was soon accomplished. Anne Pottes then made a great performance of running, weeping and wailing, to get help from nearby. A few feeble attempts to revive the dead woman were made but to no avail. She was later buried without anyone expressing suspicions.

No doubt there *were* a few mutterings when Mrs Newton's husband also died soon afterwards, and probably a little tempest of disquiet when widow and widower married each other within six months of the deaths. Local gossip was probably nothing, however, when compared to the torrent of anger raging in the heart of Anne Pottes. She felt she had been cheated of what she saw as rightfully hers, namely Thomas Cash and his comfortable lifestyle. Since she was an accomplice she could not say a word or she would surely face the gallows alongside him! Thus Cash was free to enjoy the funds he had gained from his first wife and the passionate embrace of his second.

Cash stayed at Holton for another two years, but, in the time-honoured manner of murderers down the centuries, he was tormented by memories of the dreadful deed he had committed. Just as in Zola's famous novel, *Therese Raquin,* the whole house seemed haunted by the presence of the dead spouse and Cash was unable even to stay in the room where she had died.

After two years of misery he moved to Long Oarsbie (now known as Owersby), where he lived with his second wife until she died in about 1595. He married again, to Jennet Mowse, had two children and moved to Middle Rasen in about 1599. By this stage he must have thought himself free of the crime he had committed.

Meanwhile Anne Pottes despairing of getting what she had hoped for moved to London. In 1606 as she lay ill and dying in Shoreditch she decided to unburden herself to a minister. She confessed everything. Because this was an unofficial confession, the minister was able to pass on all the details and the High Sheriff of Lincolnshire, who happened to be visiting London at the time, soon heard of it and Cash was arrested in November 1606.

Questioned by Sir William Wray, Cash confessed all and was sent to Lincoln Castle, before being executed. He had lived for a quarter of a century after the murder until the word of a dying woman had brought vengeful and terrible justice to his door.

Macabre Deeds by Firelight: Bourne, 1604

The second of these cautionary tales concerns John Dillworth, a 42 year old wheelwright from Bourne. Once more it was the unhappiness of marriage that provoked murder, although on this occasion the crime was motivated more by bad temper than by lustfulness. Dillworth was married to a much younger woman, by whom he had three children, but their life was far from one of domestic harmony. To all her friends and neighbours Mrs Dillworth appeared 'mild and gentle in all her speeches and gestures,' but when the door of their home was closed she turned into a different person entirely. 'To her husband she was another manner of woman ... the most part of her words to him were sharp, bitter and biting.'

Perhaps because of this behaviour, John started to spend most of his time in the ale house, or maybe it was his frequent absences that caused his wife to be harsh towards him! Whatever the reason, he became known as a drunkard and would rather buy drink than food for his children.

One night, after returning from the local hostelry, she gave him a piece of her mind, putting him in a foul temper. Angered by the alcohol, he struck her under the ear and she fell to the ground. Once down, he hit her twice more with the spoke of a wheel.

Mrs Dillworth never got up again, but John was not in a mood to go to the gallows for beating his wife to death. He made up the fire with wood, turfs and shavings so that it raged, then hung up curtains at the window so no one passing could wonder at the need to stoke the fire in the dead of night. He dragged his wife's body across the floor and put her on the flames, hoping that all trace of her would be gone by morning. Instead the fire went out and he was left with some grisly half-burnt remains as morning began to dawn.

Knowing that the children would soon be waking, Dillworth dragged the charred body out into the yard and hid it under a pile of thatch. He then spent the day looking after the children having no doubt told everyone that their mother had 'gone out', and began a second effort to burn her when the little ones were back in bed. But Dillworth made a fatal error – he forgot to drape the curtains across the window this time.

The smell and the light of the raging fire attracted the attention of the Town Watch, who came knocking at the door to check that everything was all right. Sensing that something underhand was taking place, the Watch broke down the door and demanded to know where Mrs Dillworth had gone – 'Why, there is all that is left of her,' her husband told them, gesturing to the fireplace.

Dillworth was unrepentant before the coroner, confessing to the murder but claiming that he had done God and the world a service 'in sending so unquiet a creature out of it.' He was sent off to Lincoln Castle in June 1604, but continued to claim he had done the right thing until his trial in August when he was convicted and taken back to Bourne for execution. Dillworth was hanged at his own front door then his body hung in chains nearby. It is hard to imagine what this must have done to his children, but the pamphleteers hoped the story would encourage husbands and wives to be more pleasant to each other.

Murdered in Bed: Kyme, 1682

The third tale concerns a Roman Catholic who committed a murder in Kyme in 1682. In the highly-charged religious atmosphere of the time the fact of the murderer's religion was taken as very significant and he was duly recorded in a Protestant pamphlet as somehow being 'typical' of Roman Catholics in general.

Mr Sherburn of Kyme seems to have been an unremarkable farmer and cattle dealer who had been happily married for 20 years. Outwardly, he lived the life of a prosperous and confident farmer, although his religious views would have isolated him from at least some of the local community. It seems nobody was aware of the storms that raged inside his head and which, one fateful night, poured out in a sudden tornado of anger directed against the nearest available person.

One night in December 1682, Mr Sherburn attacked his wife while she was asleep in bed. The story goes that he throttled her, trampled on her, and struck blows to the 'stomach and bowels.' Finally, he 'beat the breath out of her body and killed her'. It was clearly not a planned and premeditated attack, for Sherburn simply beat her to death and then left her lying there.

Not knowing what to do, Sherburn left her dead in the bed and went to sleep in another room. When morning came he still did not know what to do. This inactivity seems to suggest that

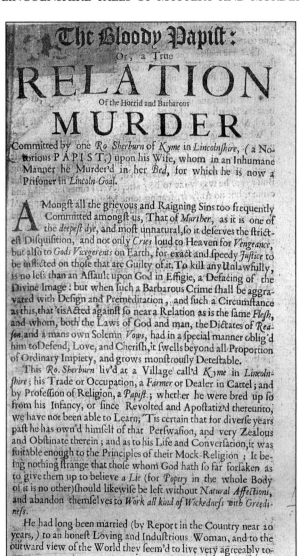

The Bloody Papist:
Or, a True

RELATION
Of the Horrid and Barbarous

MURDER

Committed by one *Ro Sherburn* of *Kyme* in *Lincolnshire*, (a Notorious P A P I S T,) upon his Wife, whom in an Inhumane Manner he Murder'd in her *Bed*, for which he is now a Prisoner in *Lincoln-Goal*.

AMongst all the grievous and Raigning Sins too frequently Committed amongst us, That of *Murther*, as it is one of the *deepest dye*, and most unnatural, so it deserves the strictest Disquisition, and not only *Cries* loud to Heaven for *Vengeance*, but also to *Gods Vicegerents* on Earth, for exact and speedy *Justice* to be inflicted on those that are Guilty of it. To kill any Unlawfully, is no less than an Assault upon God in Effigie, a Defacing of the Divine Image: but when such a Barbarous Crime shall be aggravated with Design and Premeditation, and such a Circumstance as this, that 'tis Acted against so near a Relation as is the same *Flesh*, and whom, both the Laws of God and man, the Dictates of *Reason*, and a mans own Solemn *Vows*, had in a special manner oblig'd him to Defend, Love, and Cherish, it swells beyond all Proportion of Ordinary Impiety, and grows monstrously Detestable.

This *Ro. Sherburn* liv'd at a Village call'd *Kyme* in *Lincolnshire*; his Trade or Occupation, a *Farmer* or Dealer in Cattel; and by Profession of Religion, a *Papist*.; whether he were bred up so from his Infancy, or since Revolted and Apostatiz'd thereunto, we have not been able to Learn; 'Tis certain that for diverse years past he has own'd himself of that Perswasion, and very Zealous and Obstinate therein; and as to his Life and Conversation, it was suitable enough to the Principles of their Mock-Religion; It being nothing strange that those whom God hath so far forsaken as to give them up to believe *a Lie* (for *Popery* in the whole Body of it is no other) should likewise be left without *Natural Affections*, and abandon themselves to *Work all kind of Wickedness with Greediness*.

He had long been married (by Report in the Country near 20 years,) to an honest Loving and Industrious Woman, and to the outward view of the World they seem'd to live very agreeably together

A   gethe

The Kyme murder of 1682 was publicised by anti-Catholics at a time of strong religious controversy. This is an extract from one of the pamphlets

he was struck with some form of emotional disorder or depression. The Catholic community would later try to defend him by arguing that he had been ill when younger and that he suffered from a long standing nervous disorder.

Eventually neighbours began to wonder why they had seen nothing of Sherburn or his wife and came round to look. They eventually broke into the house where the dead woman was found, still in bed. The farmer had had plenty of time to hide her body or make up an excuse about what had happened. If he had faked a robbery by travelling villains, people would probably have believed him. In the event, Sherburn was arrested and taken to the magistrates where he confessed to the killing. He was taken to Lincoln Castle for the inevitable trial and eventual execution in 1683. But there was never a satisfactory explanation as to why he killed his wife. One idea put forward was that they had rowed over ten shillings, whilst his friends claimed that Sherburn suffered from 'frantic fits'. We will never know the truth, so we must simply consider this one of those random and purposeless murders.

Whether these stories had any effect on their audience is hard to say, but they must have caused married couples to look twice at their spouse, and perhaps keep a discreet distance during heated arguments.

THE CASE OF THE LEGLESS MURDERER

———————— ✿ ————————

The year 1952 was one of optimism for many people. A new queen was on the throne and the misery and hardship of the war years was starting to fade. Some rationing had been abandoned at last, whilst up and down the country great progress was being made on building the new homes for the next generation to live in and to raise their families.

John Docherty and Sybil Hoy seemed to be ideally placed to be a successful part of that next generation. The young couple, from Felling in County Durham, were engaged to be married and had a bright future ahead of them. Sybil was 22, 'a pretty, dark-haired shop assistant', John 26, and 'a good-looking young man with light brown, wavy hair'. He had a steady job as a clerk on the Team Valley industrial estate.

But in 1952 some parts of Britain were still none too healthy and Felling, situated downstream of Gateshead on the River Tyne, was one of the most polluted. It was part of the old industrial heartlands of the northeast, a smoky mixture of coalmining, steel making and shipbuilding. The streets were narrow and cramped, and the houses small, dirty and unventilated. Disease still lurked, and one of the most feared, tuberculosis, reached out its tentacles and caught John Docherty at a time when he was least expecting it.

John was taken off to a sanatorium, an isolation hospital, leaving Sybil to worry if he would recover. After a few months, when he was judged free of infection, John was released back into the world and into the arms of his grateful fiancée. Many believed, however, that you never fully recovered from TB and that it ran in families, with men passing it on to their children. You never wanted to marry someone who had got TB, they counselled, but Sybil ignored all these stories and stood by her man.

In June 1953, when the happy couple were looking forward to their wedding, the dreaded disease struck again. Docherty experienced a renewed bout of coughing and in early 1954 the doctor sent him back to the sanatorium.

Sybil was devastated, but she also began to listen to the 'advice' of others. Life with an invalid husband would hold many complications and a young woman like Sybil had other offers to consider as well. Before long, out of sight became out of mind as other suitors emerged. In May 1954 Sybil decided to break off the engagement. She would never become Mrs Docherty.

This had a traumatic effect on Docherty. 'When my girlfriend left me and gave me the ring back, I just didn't want to live anymore,' he later said. She went further than just the ring. Sybil returned a whole series of presents that John had given her so that she would feel under no 'obligation' to him any longer. Docherty became depressed. His reason for living had gone, and he started to be moody and obsessive, most especially about Sybil.

Docherty determined he was not to be cast aside. He followed Sybil around the enclosed streets of Felling, keeping track of all of her movements. Sybil found that beginning her new life without him was not to be so simple as returning the ring.

One day in early August 1954, Docherty discovered that Sybil had disappeared. After a few enquiries, he ascertained that she had gone away. In fact she had decided to go elsewhere for a while in order to escape her ex-fiancé's endless attentions. But Docherty soon worked out where she had gone.

He knew that Sybil had a close friend with whom she had worked in a department store in Newcastle. This friend had got married and moved to Grantham in Lincolnshire, where she had had a baby. Sybil had been to visit once before and he thought it highly likely she would have gone there again.

On Sunday 8 August, Docherty went to Newcastle Central station, and got on the next train to Grantham. He arrived that night, and booked into an hotel near the station. Knowing only the surname of Sybil's married friend, he spent the next two days making enquiries about a young couple named Elliott who might have a friend staying with them.

Sybil Hoy was indeed staying at the home of her friend and her husband in Arnoldfield Flats. In order to justify her stay, she was doing her best to be helpful and that included looking after three-year-old Kevin Elliott. One morning, soon after Docherty's arrival, Mrs Elliott was busy in the home so Sybil decided to take Kevin out. She took him into the grounds of the flats, which were surrounded by dense woodland; beyond was the railway line to London. She put him in his pushchair, ready to go to the shops.

Upstairs in another of the flats, a Mrs Halford was attending to her domestic duties when she heard a series of terrible, heart-rending screams, clearly those of a woman in extreme distress. Not even pausing to consider whether it was safe to do so, she rushed outside to find Sybil lying face down on the grass. Kevin ran past her screaming. He ran to his mother and said, 'Someone is hitting auntie.' But it was worse than that; Sybil was dead, from multiple stab wounds.

Mrs Elliott saw Kevin's pushchair upturned in the roadway and, even more surprisingly, John Docherty, half-hidden in the undergrowth. 'What are you doing here?' she demanded. 'I stabbed her..... a few times,' he said, then turned and ran away through the bushes. Mrs Elliott was convinced he actually had the knife in his pocket at the time.

The police and a doctor were called. Dr Peter Maxted quickly identified four wounds on the exposed parts of the

Ernest Bond, a platelayer, found the body lying across the railway lines after the Elizabethan *express train had passed* (Lincolnshire Echo)

body, where Sybil had been stabbed in the neck and the chest. First suggestions were that 'something like a bayonet' had been used to kill her. Later studies showed she had been stabbed a total of 19 times, including three wounds to the heart.

A few hundred yards away a gang of platelayers were at work on the main London to Edinburgh railway line that passed through Grantham. Ganger Ernest Bond signalled to his colleagues a warning that one of the fastest trains, the *Elizabethan*, was approaching, so they all stopped work to stand back and watch it race by. It whistled past at about 70mph but as it did so, they saw a man dart out from the trackside, right in front of the train.

A moment of horror transfixed the men . 'Almost as soon as it [the train] had passed we saw what looked like a bundle on the line.... but it was moving,' one of them said later. First to react was Jack Stray. He got on his bike and rode 300 yards up the track to where the body lay. He found a well-dressed man, terribly injured but alive, who raised his head slightly and asked for water. The wheels of the train had cut off both his legs. An ambulance was called and the young survivor was taken to Grantham hospital.

It was not long before the brutal murder at Arnotsfield Flats was connected with the attempted suicide on the railway line nearby. The police began a frantic search for the murder weapon and concentrated their efforts on the area between the flats and the railway line, even using mine detectors. It was 26 hours before a bloodhound discovered the knife.

On 12 August the Lincolnshire papers were full of the terrible murder and reported the adjourned inquest into the death of Sybil Hoy. Meanwhile Docherty underwent surgery at Grantham hospital and soon began to recover. When he was fit enough, the police returned. At 9.30am on 26 August Detective Constable Felgate arrived at his bedside and formally charged him with the murder of Sybil Hoy. 'Tha's true,' Docherty

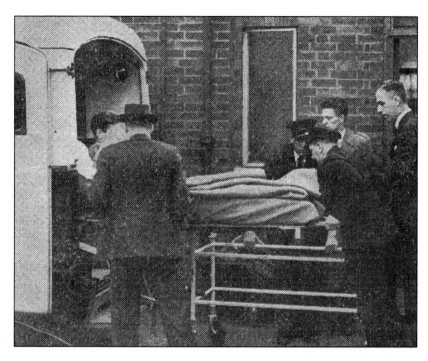

John Docherty covers his face as he is carried to a waiting ambulance at Grantham Borough hospital (Lincolnshire Echo)

replied. He was taken into custody and appeared soon afterwards for a special sitting of the Grantham magistrates at the Guildhall. News of the event had spread rapidly, so 'a large crowd of bystanders, including many women with prams and shopping bags', were waiting to see Docherty. He was brought into the Guildhall in his wheelchair, with a blanket draped across his waist and upper legs.

The hearing before the magistrates lasted a mere four minutes, after which Docherty was remanded in custody and taken to Lincoln. 'Legless man is charged with Lincs Murder' announced the *Chronicle*, and Docherty became tagged with this label from that time on.

The 'legless murderer' appeared in court again a few days later. He was remanded in custody once more and scheduled for trial in November. By this stage Docherty had made a full confession to the police, explaining how he had tracked the young woman to Grantham, found where she was staying, and then waited in the bushes until he got the chance to kill her. People were shocked that he had shown no concern for the child in the pushchair when he slaughtered Sybil. He also admitted to attempted suicide, then a crime in itself, and said that he had deliberately laid down in front of the train. Meanwhile the landlord of the inn, where he had stayed, made a brisk profit from letting out the room he had used to thrill-seekers.

Docherty's trial at Lincoln Assizes must have been one of the shortest on record, lasting just three minutes. He was carried up the steps into the dock in the arms of a prison warder and just about the only words he spoke were, 'I plead guilty my lord.' The Judge then read out the mandatory death sentence, after which Docherty placed his arms round the warder's neck so he could be carried back down the steps.

Docherty's execution was fixed for 23 November, but early that month a plea for mercy was sent to the Home Secretary. This was carefully considered, and on 15 November it was announced that the 'legless murderer' had been reprieved. He was to serve a life sentence instead.

DOUBLE MURDER ON THE HIGHWAY

————————❁————————

The 18th century was the heyday of the highwayman, when mysterious horsemen terrorised glamorous yet submissive ladies into handing over their precious jewels at the point of a pistol. These anti-heroes of the open road were, supposedly, brave and fearless in the way they intercepted stagecoaches and, if caught, went to the gallows. The newspapers of 1733 included regular reports on the lines of, 'On Saturday last the Hammersmith Stagecoach was robbed by a single highwayman between Kensington and Knightsbridge.'

Of course the reality was not at all romantic. Travellers in remote country areas ran the grim risk of being waylaid in isolated places miles from help.

Many of these villainous deeds were carried out by ordinary thugs, who lurked in hedges and ditches, not the Dick Turpin types. It was in this atmosphere of rural lawlessness that two Lincolnshire brothers committed an atrocious pair of murders that showed there was nothing romantic about highway robbery.

The Post Master at Lincoln in 1732 was a Mr Rans, who had a few problems with one of his servants, Isaac Hallam. Clearly unsuited to his job, Hallam was a man who kept bad company and could not be trusted with money. Somehow he ended up spending what was not his, and Rans must have helped him out because eventually Hallam owed him the considerable sum (for those days) of five pounds. This was many months' wages and

Gibbet Hill between Faldingworth and Market Rasen remains a lonely place

when it was not paid back, Isaac Hallam was imprisoned for debt on the instruction of Rans.

A debtors' gaol was not a pleasant place, and a prisoner depended on his friends to feed and support him whilst being denied the ability to earn the money to clear his debts. A friendless man could stay there for years, but eventually Hallam was released after some friends paid five pounds for him. Hallam swore vengeance on his erstwhile employer, but first decided to try a wider world than provincial Lincoln. He took himself off to London with his brother Thomas, where he hoped to find another job.

Hallam's London plans must have borne no fruit, because by the end of December 1732 he was trudging the weary miles back to Lincolnshire. He seems to have got by through robbery with whatever violence was necessary, along the Great North

Road. As any of these offences would have carried a death penalty if caught, he was returning to Lincolnshire a marked man. When Hallam was following the 'High Dyke' road towards Ancaster in the company of Thomas, the pair spotted a lonely traveller on horseback. A man on a horse ought to have been at an advantage when encountering suspicious strangers, but there were ways and means of un-horsing the unsuspecting traveller. The poor man was duly robbed of his money and his horse in an efficient manner.

About two hours later, a 19-year-old youth named Wright met the pair whilst driving a light, open carriage in which he had taken a Mr Thompson to Ancaster. Wright, who came from Rasen, took pity when he saw the two men uncomfortably seated on one poor horse and offered to give them a lift to Lincoln. It would have been a lengthy journey of two hours or more and to pass the time Wright chatted merrily about his comings and goings along the road. He then bade his companions farewell at Lincoln, where he stayed for a couple of days, before returning home to Rasen.

Once in Lincoln, Isaac Hallam seems to have visited his old employer, Rans, and 'had words'. He left in a fury, again swearing vengeance, and set out with his brother on the road to Market Rasen. On December 31st they lay in wait just outside Lincoln for Rans' post-boy, Thomas Gardner, to ride along. As he passed, they caught him, dragged him off his horse and murdered him by cutting his throat from 'ear to ear' and then did the same to his horse! This act alone suggests that they were motivated by vengeance rather than money because the could have sold the horse for profit. The post-boy was later buried at Nettleham, where a story grew up that the grass would not grow around his grave. This is a common legend that attaches itself to some infamous gravestones, and is more probably related to the tramp of curious feet than any mystical significance!

After murdering Rans' post-boy, the two brothers determined to rob and murder their erstwhile benefactor, young Mr Wright. During the course of the journey to Lincoln, Wright had told them that he planned to go on to Rasen later and so the two villains lay in wait for him at a remote spot near (as the *Mercury* described it) 'Fardenworth' Gate for two days. Could they have simply hidden out in the countryside in the depths of winter, or did they have a friendly home to go to at night?

Meanwhile, Wright set out on his journey home. Lincoln was an hour or two back and he had passed through Faldingworth, the last village before he reached the Rasens. He probably wished that he had left Lincoln earlier, for it was nearly five o' clock and pretty dark. Only fools and brave men travelled at night and he still had four or five miles of open, desolate countryside to negotiate before reaching the safety of home. He guided the horse round the first sharp bend north of Faldingworth and onto a stretch of straight road that ran along a low ridge between hedges.

Suddenly a figure lurched out of the darkness and grabbed at the horse's bridle, stopping the slow progress of the open chaise instantly. In one swift-movement, Wright was struck a savage blow, dragged to the ground and left for dead.

Their evil work complete, the brothers paused to survey their savage handiwork. One of them drew out his knife again and in the darkness he cut away at poor Wright's leg. Finally, the two hauled Wright's corpse up into a seated position, then lifted it back onto the chaise and placed the seat cloth across his legs. They then disappeared into the night, leaving Wright looking as if he had simply dozed off during his long ride.

The two murders astonished the county and, for many weeks after, was 'the chief subject of writing and conversation'. The Hallam brothers had disappeared. They were clearly adept travellers as they passed around the country with ease. A reward of £40 was offered in the name of William Thompson of Great Marlborough Street in London but nothing more was heard for nearly three weeks. Then they were arrested in

The Sheriff's procession assembles at Lincoln Castle, 1845
(The Illustrated London News)

Shropshire for robbery. In early February the Lincoln gaoler, Mr Wood, was despatched to Shrewsbury where both brothers made 'ample confession' to their crimes.

Arrangements were made to bring them back to Lincoln for trial and, to the delight of the *Stamford Mercury*, the pair were lodged in the George there overnight. A reporter was able to speak with them, or their gaolers, and confirm that they both admitted their crimes. Isaac Hallam was apparently concerned about Wright who, he said, had died bravely, but Thomas was not bothered at all by what he had done. Their only real regret seems to have been that they had not killed Rans: 'Mr Rans was so much in their favour, that they said they should have died with Pleasure, had they dispatched him.' When they were brought into Lincoln they were jeered by the post-boys of the area sounding loud blasts on their horns. Apparently one of the Hallams was seen to weep.

The Hallam brothers were tried at Lincoln Assizes in March 1733. It was reportedly Isaac who had taken the lead in the murders. He took the view it was best to kill anyone they robbed, because robbery was a capital offence anyway. They confessed to 63 robberies and one other murder, but also made attempts to escape from the captivity of their irons using a knife notched like a saw and a spike nail.

On 16th March the pair were taken out to be executed and hung in chains. Isaac was the first to be dealt with at the spot where he had killed the post-boy near Lincoln. On reaching the site of Gardner's murder, Isaac Hallam was at last hit by the terror of his situation and fell into 'violent agonies'. There was no clergyman present to offer spiritual support, however, and his only comfort was from a spectator who helped him pray. Thomas broke into shrieks when he saw his brother die.

After this, Thomas was taken to Faldingworth Gate to be executed for the murder of Wright. The place remained famous for its gibbet for many years afterwards. Some old maps labelled the spot 'Gibbet Hill', and it remains a lonely and windswept spot to this day.

FLIGHT INTO NOWHERE

———————— ❁ ————————

To the casual observer, the 8th/9th September 1970 must have seemed like a normal evening of activity at RAF Binbrook, the fighter station that sat in the Lincolnshire Wolds near Louth. Captain William Schaffner, a 28-year-old American pilot working with the RAF squadron, climbed into the cockpit of his Lightning jet fighter, XS894, and prepared for another of the Cold War sorties out over the North Sea.

His departure, however, was rather hasty.

According to some reports, Schaffner did not bother to complete the usual pre-flight checks and failed to sign the forms to indicate he was happy with the aircraft. He left so abruptly that, according to one airman, who was in the Binbrook Flying Clothing section, he did not even take the anti-g suit, which helped to protect against blacking out. Even more unusually, Schaffner ordered the crew to stop the refuelling before the tank was full and started the engines without warning, disregarding the Ground Marshal. Subsequently when Schaffner took off into the night sky he was less prepared than he should have been.

As the ground crew watched the plane disappear into the darkness and head out to the North Sea, perhaps they wondered if, for once, this was a real emergency rather than one of the endless games they played as training exercises. None of them could have guessed though, that this was to be Schaffner's last flight. His disappearance into the grey waters of the North Sea triggered international tales of flying saucers and alien abduction that are still being discussed 30 years on.

The late 60s early 70s was a time of heightened tension in the Cold War. For the pilots and radar technicians who guarded the eastern coast of England, this meant constant awareness of probing flights by Russian airmen. They also needed to be on the look out for spy ships in various guises heaving their way through the choppy waters. A network of radar stations and observation posts kept a vigilant watch day and night so it was perhaps inevitable that, eventually, people would begin to report that they had seen *something* in the night sky.

According to the UFO believers, the events which led to Schaffner's disappearance, went something like this. On 8th September a radar trace which was unrecognisable as Soviet aircraft was picked up at the Saxa Vord station. The trace appeared on screens at 37,000 feet and appeared to be travelling

William Schaffner

at an incredible 900mph. This caused considerable alarm, especially when the object vanished off the screens, only to reappear somewhere else moments later. Lightning aircraft were scrambled to go and have a look, but it seemed unlikely that anyone could actually intercept such a fast-moving object. When the planes began to approach, the trace vanished from the radar screens, and then reappeared just off the coast of Denmark!

It was decided that further assistance was required. So at 9.45pm RAF Binbrook received a request to send another Lightning into the sky to join those already on patrol. Captain Schaffner was the pilot on call and the speed of his departure indicates the degree of concern in top-level ranks.

Schaffner took off at 10.06pm and headed up the coast to a rendezvous off Whitby.

What happened next depends rather on what evidence you believe. There are those who are certain that Schaffner made contact with aliens. Their evidence is an alleged flight transcript logging the calls that the American pilot made. Schaffner's first report was that he had made 'visual contact' with the strange craft, which he described as giving off a bluish but very bright light. Although it was so bright that it hurt his eyes, Schaffner was able to make out a conical shape. He also reported another object close by, 'Something else … like a large soccer ball,' which he thought seemed to be made of a glass-like material.

Schaffner then reported that one of the objects had turned towards him and he radioed that he was taking evasive action. Radio operators had now lost contact, but the radar technician saw two blips, which had been moving at 500mph, merge into one and become stationary. After a couple of minutes, the single radar blip suddenly accelerated up to 600mph and climbed into the sky, before splitting back into two separate blips. One of the objects then vanished off the screens at an alarming speed – estimated to be 20,400mph.

When contact was re-established with Schaffner he reported seeing lights in the sky and feeling dizzy. He also reported mechanical failure. He said the compass wasn't working and all electronic instruments had failed. The chances of him being able to return safely seemed slim. His control ordered a Shackleton rescue plane to the area and instructed Schaffner to carry out a controlled ditching in the North Sea.

The next report was from the Shackleton. It had located the Lightning, which had ditched successfully and was still in one piece. The cockpit canopy was open, but there was no sign of Schaffner. The lumbering Shackleton circled slowly round and came back for another pass over the stricken fighter. This time its crew reported that the Lightning was now sinking, but that the cockpit canopy was *closed*. The crew called for helicopter support but could not explain the position of the canopy or the

The wreckage of an RAF Lightning aircraft is retrieved from the North Sea

disappearance of Schaffner. If he had closed the canopy, where had he been when they passed over the first time; and where had he gone when they came round again?

The plane sank into the cold, dark waters of the North Sea off Flamborough Head, but a patient search located the wreckage after three weeks. Those who favour the alien theory again point to confusion in the evidence. When divers from HMS Kiddlestone first reached the wreck on 7th October they reported the pilot was still in the cockpit, but when the plane was brought to the surface the cockpit was empty!

Conspiracy theorists, who suspect an official cover-up, also point to unusual practices once the wreckage was brought to land. Wrecked planes were normally taken to Farnborough for study, but on this occasion the Lightning was taken to Binbrook. A team was summoned from Farnborough to investigate it at its home base. In a lengthy article about the case, Tony Dodd, a retired policeman with a passion for UFO reports, claimed that one of these aircrash investigators subsequently became his informant. He told Dodd that the wreck was placed beneath a tarpaulin and under an armed guard at Binbrook. Normally allowed free rein, the crash investigators had only rudimentary access to the plane and were supervised by five civilians, including two Americans.

The informant also said that all the plane's instruments, such as compass, voltmeter and direction indicators, had been removed and a different ejector seat had been fitted. This would seem to make any disputes over whether the ejector seat had been faulty and how the cockpit canopy came to be moved worthless. There was a revolting smell in the cockpit and the plane was also slimy after its weeks in the sea. After a brief investigation, the plane was taken away to an airbase at Kirkland in the USA. An unusual move, justified by saying that the pilot had been American.

Tony Dodd and other UFO enthusiasts maintain that the authorities covered up the truth about what had really happened to William Schaffner. A detailed website attempts to provide evidence for the alien abduction theory making this one of the most-discussed Lincolnshire mysteries of recent years. Dodd states that he obtained access to transcripts of the officer's in-flight conversations after clandestine meetings on York railway station and in a lay-by off the A1. One contact, however, who knew all about the incident, died in apparently mysterious circumstances. He crashed his car while drunk, even though he was reputed never to touch alcohol.

The disappearance of Schaffner came at a time when other attributed UFO sightings were occurring off the Lincolnshire coast. Indeed, it is claimed that the whole might of NATO was harnessed into 'Operation Aeneid' after a huge, 180ft long UFO, surrounded by numerous glass-like ball objects, had been sighted at Donna Nook on the Lincolnshire coast. The object had apparently spent several hours over the bombing range and had been observed by several RAF men. There were also reports of huge triangular objects, which dived straight into the sea, thus becoming USOs, Unidentified Submarine Objects! More of this in chapter 10. This has encouraged beliefs among many that the authorities know a lot more about UFOs than they allow the general public to know

It has been persistently argued that Schaffner had actually been kidnapped by aliens and interest in the story was such that it built up a life of its own, leading to further investigation by the BBC and others. Official documents came to light, which showed that Schaffner had simply been attempting to intercept another aircraft, but had flown too low and hit the sea. 'It was a tragic accident and there is no other explanation,' was the official summary.

The latest documents to be revealed show the official explanation to be that Schaffner had left on a practice interception exercise. The target was a Shackleton aircraft which would have been much slower-moving than his own Lightning and was flying at only 1500 feet and 160 knots. For some reason the Shackleton lost radio contact and had no sight of the Lightning until, by the light of a flare, they saw it beneath them in the sea. It was argued that Schaffner had not been properly trained for this sort of mission, had tried to intercept the Shackleton from beneath and not been able to eject properly. He had probably made a misjudgement when trying to decelerate in order to get the correct angle for the interception, and did not realise how much altitude he had lost.

Yet the arguments refuse to die down. Schaffner's disappearance left plenty of unexplained details, such as his over-hasty departure for a 'training' mission. Arguments still continue about how Schaffner supposedly closed the cockpit after getting out of the plane, and how it came to be in the water with so little damage. For the time being, though, it remains a mystery which has enough strange elements to support the theory that extra-terrestrial activity was involved.

DEATH AT THE FARM

———————❀———————

On a drab Saturday morning in October 1931, James Jacklin left his home in Waddingham early as usual and began his routine cycle ride across the lonely Lincolnshire landscape for the mile or two to his son's farm at Holmes. It was a quiet spot at the best of times and Mr Jacklin would have had plenty of time on his ride to collect his thoughts for the coming day. It was a route he took every day, for the farm was run as a partnership between father and son, although the widowed farmer had given up the farmhouse for his son's young family.

It had turned out to be a difficult year for many in the area, including the farmers, and money was short. Three years before Robert Jacklin had married a local girl called Annie Priscilla Codd, whose father had been the village carrier at Waddingham and then done a bit of farming himself over at Springthorpe. Now there was an eighteen-month-old baby to feed, as well as a sixteen-year-old nephew, Harold Smith. He had helped on the farm since January. Harold had previously lived with old Mr Jacklin, but now he slept in a room next to the younger Jacklin.

Perhaps James was thinking about Harold as he cycled to Holmes Farm. Things had turned out badly with the boy who often quarrelled with his son and had even run off once.

Mr Jacklin reached the farmyard at about half past seven, by which time folks were usually up and about. He noticed that the bedroom window was open, but then his attention was diverted by the open door of the coalhouse. That was where his son usually kept his own bike, but this morning it wasn't there.

He walked up to the door of the farmhouse and found it locked. When he knocked there was no reply. Concern began to change into worry, even fear. He could smell smoke, like burning straw, and from upstairs there was the sound of the baby crying. He banged on the door with no response from inside, apart from the insistent cries of 'Mama' from the baby. Mr Jacklin decided to break down the door and what he found inside shocked the whole country.

The kitchen was cloudy with whisps of smoke. Across the stone floor was a rug, and straw had been spread on it. This was smouldering as if someone had made an attempt to set light to it. There was even an old pair of trousers, left there in a pathetic attempt – it would seem – to build a small fire. He

The farmhouse at Waddington Holme – the scene of an horrific double murder. The cross indicates the window from which Robert seems to have tried to escape or call out (Lincolnshire Echo)

called out, but there was no reply except the sound of the baby still crying upstairs. He followed the noise upstairs and into the young couple's bedroom to be met by a scene of awful devastation. No doubt his first glance was to his grandson in his cot, but then he took in the scene on the bed.

'Whatever is the matter?' the old man said, as the figure of his son seemed to rise up slightly in the bed. 'I don't know,' Robert replied with a voice that sounded strangely different, then collapsed down onto the blankets.

There was blood everywhere and, in the middle of the bed, Annie Jacklin lay dead. Beside her lay her badly wounded husband, clearly dying, 'with part of his face shot away.' His jaw and nose had been almost completely blasted away by a shotgun fired at close range. There was blood across the floor and blood around the open window as if someone had made a vain attempt to call for help.

Horrified, old Mr Jacklin asked his son what had happened. 'I don't know,' he replied, before collapsing again. Mr Jacklin must have suspected murderous burglars had broken in during the night. But where was young Harold? No time to answer such questions for now, he had to get help for his son and medical help would be hard to find.

Annie Jacklin was probably asleep when she was shot through the mouth and killed instantly. Robert had been shot through the right cheek and also had pellets in his arm which, crucially, showed that his wounds were not self-inflicted. Stories of depressed farmers killing themselves were all too familiar in those difficult days. Robert was taken to Lincoln County Hospital where he spoke again, briefly, to a nurse. 'I was in bed with my wife,' he said, 'I cannot remember anything until I came to this place.' He said nothing else and died two days later.

Superintendent Dolby was called out to Holmes Farm to investigate this terrible incident. People were already discussing their own theories. The young farmer had shot his wife and then turned his gun on himself was one theory. A gang of wandering thieves had raided the farm and killed the young couple after a desperate struggle was another. But others pointed to the disappearance of the young nephew, Harold, and of Robert's bike.

Dolby found a trail of blood around the bedroom window and also down the wall outside. This indicated that someone, presumably Robert, had leant out and tried to call for help after being shot. A candle had been left burning at the bedside and the candlestick was spattered with blood. An attempt to call for help ruled out further the murder-and-suicide theory, as did the position of the murder weapon. The childish attempt to set fire to the house and the missing bike, also implied a third party. There were also two spent cartridges on the floor, which had been removed from the shotgun, and the locked door downstairs, which was also odd. Would burglars have really locked the door on their way out?

A search of the area around the farm led to a strange discovery under a gorse bush. A box was found containing a pair of trousers, a cheque for £12 and some money. Possibly the murderer had tried to cycle off on Jacklin's bike with the box, found it too difficult, and so hidden it.

An alert was sent out to try and trace Harold Smith, but he had already vanished into the Lincolnshire autumn. He was described as being five feet seven inches with protruding teeth and walked 'with a slovenly gait.'

Harold Smith's family came from Scawby Brook so the search concentrated on that area. This was a remote, sparsely populated area of small villages and dispersed farms, many of which were not on the telephone. All the police could do was to watch the roads and towns, waiting for a sighting of a boy on a bike. Some time between nine and ten o'clock that Saturday night, the police received a report of a young man riding a bike two miles outside Brigg on the road to Wrawby. In order to catch up, PC Smith commandeered a motor lorry[1]

---

1. Also described as a bus in another report.

James Jacklin and Superintendent Dolby of the Brigg police
(Lincolnshire Echo)

and gave chase. At half past ten he had no trouble arresting Harold who was riding his uncle's bike.

Harold was charged at Brigg Magistrates' Court the next Monday evening. It is said, he walked unconcernedly into the dock, by which time news of the brutal killings had spread far and wide, albeit not always accurately. 'The discovery of a farmer and his wife dying shot in the bedroom and the kitchen floor covered with smouldering straw, was made at Waddingham near Brigg on Saturday morning,' wrote one journalist. Amidst all the excitement, though, details got confused. The same report stated that a double-barrelled shotgun had been found on the bedroom floor and also that no weapon had been found!

With all the press coverage, quite a crowd gathered to see the youthful suspect, as well as a host of eager reporters. 'A tall, fair-haired youth, smart in appearance, Smith stepped lightly into the dock and appeared to take little interest in the proceedings,' the *Lincolnshire Chronicle* wrote. While an inquest into the death of Mrs Jacklin was held in the parlour at Holmes Farm, Robert Jacklin was breathing his last in Lincoln Hospital.

The court appearance gave Harold Smith the first chance to tell his story in public. This included a number of changes of direction and confused attempts to shift the blame elsewhere, yet at the same time he also admitted that he had shot both the Jacklins. At first, Harold almost seemed to be making it out to have been some form of accident. 'I touched the trigger and the gun went off and shot Mr Jacklin first. The missus looked up and I shot her as well,' he said. To try and get a clear picture, Harold was encouraged to explain the background to the incident and a picture of brooding bitterness and resentment gradually emerged.

It became clear that his relationship with Robert Jacklin had not been good. After one row, he had run off to a Mr Green until his own father had brought him back to Holmes Farm. On this occasion he had been expecting to get into further trouble when he failed to put straw in the henhouse as he had been told. This fear of further censure seems to have tipped him over the edge. 'I have been going to do it ever so many times. I ought to have shot myself as well,' Harold told the magistrates. He said he had got out of bed at about half-past four in the morning, got the shotgun and cartridges, and then climbed the stairs. He had stood outside the Jacklins' door for four or five minutes, wondering whether or not to do away with them. He had then gone into their room, still uncertain what he would do. Then the gun had gone off and he had shot Robert first, followed by his wife.

Harold tried to explain the fire next, which he had attempted to light with a candle, the rug and some old trousers in order to hide what had happened. Of course this was incriminating material, for Harold was effectively explaining that he knew what he was doing and had, rationally, tried to cover his tracks.

He next told the court that he had ridden off on Mr Jacklin's bike via Scawby and Brigg to Worlaby, where he stopped to buy a newspaper. At Weston he managed to get a job for the day as a milkman with a Mr Farrow, having supplied a reference that he had written for himself. After his rambling story, Harold pleaded 'not guilty', but the magistrates sent him to the Crown Court on a charge of murder in any case. In fact by the end of the evening it had become two murders.

The sombre atmosphere continued to the Wednesday, when the funerals of the two victims were held at the tiny Primitive Methodist chapel in Waddingham. In keeping with tradition, the blinds were drawn on every house in the village as the cortege passed by. Robert and Annie were laid to rest in the same grave in the village churchyard.

Harold Smith's case quickly came to court and he was tried in Lincoln at the start of November. He was only tried for the murder of Mrs Jacklin, the other murder charge being left to 'lie upon the calendar'. He made a last, feeble attempt to blame the murders on someone else by saying that he had been woken in the night by a shot. When he had gone up to the room, Robert Jacklin had the gun at his side and his hand resting on it. He said that he had made up his earlier confession. Neither the burglary nor suicide story could explain, however, why he had ridden off on his employer's bike and got himself a new job. There was discussion of the motive, but few could get further than the bad feeling that had existed between the boy and Robert Jacklin over the low wages and shoddy work. The farm, the court was told, 'was not doing very well'.

Mr Joy had the task of defending Smith, which he did by suggesting that Jacklin had been a harsh employer. He implied that six pence a week was almost a slave wage and raised the fact that Jacklin father and son had taken each other to court in the past. Robert Jacklin was a 'surly and depressed' character, he suggested.

This left the jury of 'rough countrymen' to decide on the fate of young Harold, and it was a task that they found most dreadful. 'Tears rolled down the ruddy faces of some ... while others blew their noses vigorously and furtively wiped their eyes,' a journalist reported. But the verdict of guilty was inevitable, although the jury entered a plea of mercy, and this was followed quickly by Justice Mackinnon pronouncing sentence of death. 'Smith heard the death sentence unmoved, turned smartly and with a firm step walked down the stairs to the cells.'

Eventually, though, Smith's age saved him from the gallows. The appeal launched by Counsel was sufficient to secure a reprieve from the death sentence. The new Home Secretary, Sir Herbert Samuel, chose not to insist on the first execution of an under-18 in over 40 years. Smith's life was spared, even though he had taken two and left a small child orphaned.

BLACK DOGS AND OTHER STRANGE BEASTS

————————— ✿ —————————

There have been many accounts of strange animal sightings in Lincolnshire over the years, including the occasional dragon! Yet the most persistent visitor seems to be the black dog, which haunts the lanes and byways of every corner of the county.

It has been suggested that these ghostly dogs may be connected with an old Lincolnshire tradition of burying a dog in medieval houses as some form of protection against spirits. One example of this is the apparent sighting of a black dog with a woman's face, seen at the site of an old cottage in Knaith.

So what do these dogs look like? Most of those who claim to have seen one have thought they were real dogs, until some strange spectral behaviour occurred.

One story goes back to Victorian times when a lady was passing near the fishpond at Blyborough near Gainsborough. These ponds were once a common feature of the landscape, but many have been filled in and ploughed over. While the lady tarried near the fishpond, perhaps looking into its murky waters in search of a fish or a frog, she saw a dog lolloping around. She described it as black, not too clean, of indeterminate breed, and certainly not a 'gentleman's dog'. Deciding it was time to go, she quietly moved away from the pond and into the lane, hoping the dog would not notice her.

But the black dog chased after her. As he came bounding up behind her, she clutched at the only weapon she had, her

Blyborough ponds, scene of a legendary appearance of the black dog

umbrella. Gripping it tightly, she swiped out and down at the black dog as it came panting towards her. Though the dog was close, she felt no impact, so she hit out again. Imagine her horror when she saw the umbrella pass clean through the dog, which continued bounding and jumping besides her!

In fact her excited companion was not at all put off by her hostile attitude, and followed her along the lane. The maddened woman continued with her futile attempts to ward the dog off with her umbrella until, eventually, the animal tired of its sport and vanished into a field.

In the mid-1800s a character called Sammy Prettywell is reputed to have taken a shot at the black dog, with disastrous effects. The gun burst, and Sammy could never use it again, although he was lucky to escape without injury to himself.

At Algarkirk a woman saw the dog three times. She described it as tall and thin with a long neck and a pointed nose. She added the additional details that it was a creature of habit, always appearing from the left. At Gunthorpe, the black dog was described as having eyes 'as big as tea sorsers'. Despite these witnesses, another who saw a black dog at Willoughton said it was not really dog-like at all, but had a bristly skin much like a pig. This particular encounter took place in 1933 and must have been very alarming. In this instance, the creature apparently pushed its victim against a gatepost, with its paws resting on their shoulders.

The dogs seem to have had powerful attractions to particular places, such as the road up to Moortown Hall. Many people reported seeing a black dog there, but on other occasions people simply felt a dog brushing up against them without actually seeing anything. There was agreement, though, that the dog always appeared in the same part of the hedge. On one occasion the dog frightened a horse pulling a baker's van, which steadfastly refused to budge any further up the lane. In the end the baker had to get down and carry the bread to the Hall instead.

In the early 1900s a young man who cycled from Leverton to Wrangle often saw the black dog loping along on the same stretch of road whilst the appearances at Algarkirk tended to always be in a clump of three trees near the church. The Blyborough dog always appeared near the fishpond and then ran along to disappear by an ash tree, mind you, one witness said the dog actually disappeared up or *into* the tree.

One common fact is that the dog never seems to have threatened anyone. A schoolmistress who saw it between Kirton-in-Lindsey and Manton in the 1930s reported that it was just trotting along the verge of the lane.

Just west of Kirton-in-Lindsey lies Belle Hole farm, near the river Eau. The farmer, and his family knew all about the black dog for it had troubled the neighbourhood on and off for years. It may have scared the children on occasions, but it seems to have been such a regular visitor that it was more of a nuisance than a cause of terror. As a result the farmer decided to try and rid his home of the ghostly visitor.

His anti-dog campaign was rather touchingly simplistic. All dogs, the farmer reckoned, like to have somewhere to live, so he first set himself the task of following the dog and finding out where it slept. One day the dog came bounding across the fields, ran around, and then turned to bound away again. This time the farmer crept behind it, panting hard in his effort to keep up with it, or at least keep it in sight. It was hardly a fair race, for the dog's paws didn't quite seem as mired in the earth as the farmer's boots felt!

Eventually the black dog disappeared into a hole in the dyke banks of the Eau. 'Here's my chance,' the farmer thought, 'I can trap the damned beast underground!' He rushed off to get a shovel and working with the amazing energy of a man on a mission, he blocked the dyke hole up with earth. Convinced he had solved the problem, he then walked back home with a self-satisfied smirk on his face. Foolish man!

The farmer told his wife about his daring trick, no doubt expecting her to be impressed. Whatever she thought, she didn't have to keep it to herself for long. While she was mixing a cake at the kitchen table with the children all around, the black dog walked straight in as if to say hello. It didn't seem to have any resentful feelings, more an attitude of amused condescension about the futility of human efforts. After taking a good look around the kitchen, it disappeared back outside. But how did it get in and out? Did it jump through the open window, open the door by itself – or did it simply walk through the wall? A dog that could do that would hardly be restrained by a few feet of soft earth blocking its den.

Undaunted, the farmer went straight back out to make a better job of blocking the hole. Of course it did no good at all.

The one person who hadn't seen the black dog was the children's nursemaid. She seems to have been a down to earth type, always scoffing at the children's fanciful notions. She also disapproved of the parents seeming to encourage the childish imaginings. 'But Nurse,' they said one night while she was

Belle Hole farm nestles close to a prominent dip in the escarpment, a popular lair for the black dog

brushing their hair, 'we have seen the black dog. He really *does* exist, you know.'

'Tush,' laughed nurse. 'You won't fool me with those old wives' tales. This *is* the 19th century you know. I don't believe in any such dog.'

'Careful Nurse,' said the oldest child, 'he won't like it if you say that. He might come and scare you.'

'Scare *me*?' she retorted in her most impressive Nurse-style. 'I shall scare *him*. If a dirty black dog turned up here I would – I would – put him in my pocket!'

The very next day, Nurse was busying herself about the house, when she suddenly felt the hairs on the back of her neck bristle. The black dog all was standing right in front of her. All Nurse's confident rebuttal of the dog stories flooded away. She remembered what she had said about the dog, and feared he would be very angry.

The dog seemed to speak to her. 'So,' she felt him say. 'Which pocket are you going to put me in?' He looked her up and down, making her feel very *small* whereas he seemed lean and powerful. 'Hmmm,' he concluded, 'I don't think you've got a pocket big enough.' The dog almost seemed to laugh, then melted away.

Another black dog caused serious disruption at a police station 'somewhere in Lindsey' by running in and out of the station – through the walls!

In the early 1900s, there was a dog at Wrangle that was seen near a long, deep pond and was also seen at different bridges at Brigg, between Manton and Scotter and at Willingham. At Bonnewells Lane near Bransby the dog was supposed to appear near a pond mythically linked with Cromwell, who watered his horses there. There was also supposed to be a ghostly lady and some phantom pigs, which would have made an interesting sight if they all decided to appear together!

A more recent description of an encounter with a black dog is given by a Northampton academic, Simon Sherwood, who grew up in Spalding. He saw the mystical creature when he was aged between three and five, and has preserved an account he wrote about it at the age of ten:

'The year was about 1974. I had been in bed a couple of hours. I awoke to hear a patter of feet. I looked up thinking it was my dog, but to my terror I saw a massive black animal probably with horns, but perhaps ears, galloping along the landing towards my bedroom. I tried to scream but found it impossible. The creature's eyes were bright yellow and as big as saucers. The animal got to my bedroom door and then vanished as quick as it appeared. I then managed to scream and my mum came in to calm me down. She said it was a reflection of car headlights what I thought was a ghost. I believed this until a few years later when I was reading a local paper, which had an article about a haunted council house which was inhabited by a poltergeist. A variety of objects were hurled at the family's baby child. The father claimed that a black dog rushed at him and then disappeared. He also claimed that a black goat had been seen running around the house. I also thought I saw a ghostly black goat on the landing of my old house. After reading this article I was convinced that what I thought had happened a few years back had most probably happened.'

So, what are the black dogs? Are they ghostly creatures, a product of the imagination, or simply a coincidental group of wandering canines linked together solely by rumour and suggestion? They have certainly been a feature of Lincolnshire life for a very long time, going right back to the 12th century. For instance, around 1127, Henry of Poitou, who was abbot of Peterborough, saw black huntsmen with black spectral dogs in the woods near Stamford. Others have linked black dogs to the wider tradition of spirits called 'barguest', often translated as meaning 'town ghost' or 'bear ghost'.

We will probably never know, but it is worth a moment to deviate onto other strange wild animals and the story of the last Lincolnshire wild cat. By the 1840s the wild cat was believed to be extinct in Lincolnshire but parts of the county still harboured exotic wild creatures despite the best efforts of gamekeepers. Bullington Wood was one such place. In 1883 a farmer went into the wood shooting with his dog, which started chasing around to flush some creature out of its lair. Imagine the farmer's surprise when the dog suddenly turned tail and fled. Some wild and angry creature flashed past after it, before running up a tree, where the farmer promptly shot it. Out of the branches fell a 46-inch long wild cat, which weighed in at eighteen pounds. It was taken off to Lincoln to be stuffed as a prize trophy. It was certainly a great rarity, for the wild cat had been pronounced extinct in England three years earlier.

So, according to science, here was the creature that didn't really exist and perhaps our black dog falls into the same category!

A DOUBLE EXECUTION

───────❀───────

The last public execution to be performed at Lincoln Castle on 5 August 1859 was unusual in being a double execution. Two young men paid with their lives for the 'death in a sewer' murder of an elderly man near Sibsey. There was little mystery about this case, it was an inept and poorly planned murder in pursuit of small financial gain. The victim, William Stevenson, had even taken pity on one of his eventual murderers, Henry Carey, taking him in after the young man had been turned out of his own home.

In his confession, 24 year old Carey blamed his downfall on drink. Indeed, this sorry tale began in the Ship Inn at Sibsey West Fen on 17th March 1859, where Henry Carey and William Picket were sitting drinking what was left of their wealth and discussing the state of the world. They concluded that *their* world was not in a good state, whereas others seemed to have much better luck and much more money. This, to them at least, seemed an injustice.

After a while, the pair got talking about William Stevenson who was also in the pub. He was reputed to have some money in his pockets as part of a pig-dealing project. Quite which of them first came up with the idea of robbing the old man was never agreed, but it was bound to have been a risky plan concocted in an alcoholic haze. According to Picket, Carey said, 'Let's kill the old bastard, I think he's got some money.'

Both men were on the very lowest rungs of society, with no permanent home. They told the landlord that they were going to sleep the night in an old boat, and left the Ship Inn ahead of

The Stone Bridge drain at Sibsey, the most likely setting for the murder of William Stevenson in 1859

their intended victim. The plan was simple – find a dark place (quite easy at midnight in the Fens!) and rob him. Both young men then grabbed a hedge-stake each and lay down at the roadside in a highly rudimentary attempt to hide.

Stevenson had not had so much to drink that he was insensible, so as soon as he came along the lane he saw the two figures crouching at the roadside. He called out to them, suspecting that there could be no good reason for lurking on the dyke bank at night. Seeing their plan was exposed and fearing that there would be no way out of trouble, both men laid about him mercilessly with their weapons, knocking Stevenson down and striking him several times. They struck so hard that one of the stakes was broken into five pieces and the old man lapsed into unconsciousness.

After a moment's drunken confusion, they took hold of his shoulders and legs and threw Stevenson into the 'sewer' or ditch that ran alongside the lane. Whether this was meant to dispose of the body or make sure that he drowned was unclear, but it had quite the reverse effect. The cold water revived the old man and he stood up in the water, coughing and spluttering, and began struggling to clamber across the ditch and out the other side. Picket rushed over and struck the old man again, finally killing him off with the victim's own walking stick.

The two villains rifled through the dead man's pockets, hoping for rich pickings, but the takings were meagre. Picket took a sovereign, whilst Carey had eight shillings and six pence, plus a knife. They were clear-minded enough to know that this would be evidence against them if found, but still too muddled to conceive of a good plan of what to do. They sloped back to the Ship Inn where they hid the fruits of their crime in two small bags in the landlord's rubbish pit, whilst the knife was hidden near his privy.

By this time the drink was starting to have another effect on the two killers, so instead of making a hasty getaway they went for a sleep in a nearby barn. The owner of the barn, George Sands, discovered them at 5.30 am, and he was not impressed to find two drunken half-wits asleep on his property.

Stevenson's body was soon discovered and Sergeant James was called in to investigate. He found plenty of evidence of violent assault, including a pool of blood in Musgrove's Field, 15 yards from the road, and even blood splattered along the top of the roadside hedge. It was clearly murder, and it did not take long for Sergeant James to deduce what probably happened. A few simple questions uncovered the fact that the old man was going home from the pub, and it was easy to discover who else had been there that night. Picket was arrested first, then Carey, in the tap room of the Ship Inn, where he was drunk and violent, swearing abusively at the officer. Carey claimed that he was lodged at the inn all night.

The two men were taken to the scene of the crime for some elementary police work. It was found that footmarks at the

Print sellers sold 'souvenir literature' to the crowds: this one was specially adapted for a double execution

murder scene exactly matched the boots of Carey, but none matched Picket's.

At the trial in August, both accused men cut sorry figures. The *Lincolnshire Chronicle* reported that both men were 'of repulsive countenance' and noted that Carey had 'a low forehead thought to distinguish murderers'. This was the influence of the pseudo-science of phrenology, which taught that the character of a person could be understood by the shape of their head.

Carey pleaded guilty to robbery but Picket confessed the whole story and his evidence proved crucial. Both men were sentenced to hang.

Before the execution they 'fully confessed their guilt and manifested the greatest penitence,' it was reported. But remorse never saved anyone from the hangman's noose. Nor did it have a salutary effect on Carey's family, for his brother Joseph was transported to Australia eight years later.

A WOMAN ON THE SCAFFOLD

———————————— ❂ ————————————

The execution of women became increasingly rare as the 20th century progressed. Indeed only thirteen were executed in the whole country during the first half of the century. Despite this, there were still plenty of murderesses about, although many were 'recommended to mercy' and never hanged. Of 108 thus recommended in the mid-1930s, only four were executed, one of whom was an obscure middle-aged housewife from a small village in Lincolnshire.

When Ethel Major went to her death at Hull Prison on 19th December 1934, there were still some who argued that she was innocent. Many more believed there was no need for capital punishment in her case because, although she had murdered her husband, she was unlikely to kill anyone else.

Ethel Brown was born in Lincolnshire in 1891, and grew up in Tumby and Kirkby-on-Bain. She became pregnant aged nineteen, but never revealed the father's name. When the child was born she was named Auriel Iris Tryphene Brown, and raised by Ethel's parents. Auriel was passed off as Ethel's younger sister, though the great age gap must surely have aroused comment. By the time Ethel went to the gallows, history seemed to be repeating itself; Auriel was pregnant at that stage, again by an un-named lover.

Ethel eventually married Arthur Major on 1st June 1918, only five months after they met. Unkind local people commented that, at 27 and with a 'secret', she could not afford to let the chance slip.

The Majors moved to No. 2, Council Houses, Kirkby-on-Bain. They were back in the village where people knew about Ethel's past, and it was not long before Arthur discovered the secret of the earlier pregnancy. In some reports this placed a strain on their relationship from which it never recovered.

Relations between the couple became increasingly acrimonious and Mrs Major moved out of the marital bedroom. On one occasion Ethel wrote to the local police to denounce her husband for driving his lorry whilst drunk. Eventually she and her son, born five months after their wedding in 1918, took to sleeping at her father's house in Roughton whenever Mr Major was the worse for drink. Ethel then found some hidden love letters in her husband's room, which were signed 'Rose' and made mention of Auriel. Their

Mrs Major shortly before her arrest (left) and her husband Arthur Major (Lincolnshire Echo)

neighbour Mrs Kettleborough was called Rose, and so Mrs Major concluded that she must be the writer of the love letters.

In April 1934 Ethel went to see her doctor and told him that she had received an anonymous letter telling her that her husband had 'a nice bit of fluff'. She told him that her husband was not fit to live. Ethel put this accusation to Arthur, who denied it, but a fortnight later on 5th May, Ethel found a postcard addressed to him with the mysterious message, 'Meet me same place same time: baby got prize'. The following week, Ethel spoke to Rose Kettleborough's husband about her suspicions – but he denied the story out of hand.

By this time a number of anonymous letters seem to have been flying around. The Chief Constable of Lincolnshire received one on 15th May, saying that Major's employers often had their gravel lorries in use for illegally carrying passengers. It also stated that the driver was drunk. It seems likely that Mrs Major sent this letter herself, and there was always argument over the true origins of the other letters she said she had seen.

The Majors began to lead increasingly separate lives, keeping their food on different shelves for example. On one occasion Ethel was seen to chase her husband up the street, and twice stooped to pick up a brick and throw it at him.

Ethel's campaign against her husband included suggesting to Sergeant Mitchell that he was putting things in her tea to get rid of her. This was an interesting notion, given the manner of Arthur's sudden death soon after. She also began to run up debts, to the extent that Arthur contacted the local paper on 19th May to place an advertisement saying that he would not pay his wife's debts. According to some sources, Ethel was also worried that her husband would take out a summons against her for writing false letters.

Events came to a head on 22nd May 1934. Arthur Major came home after driving his lorry, had his usual tea of corned beef, and then complained of feeling ill. A short while later he had what was assumed to be a fit in the back yard. All evening he showed signs of being unusually ill. He lost the ability to speak and his legs jerked uncontrollably. Throughout all this time Mrs Major made no attempt to call the doctor until her father suggested it when he came to visit later in the evening. The doctor arrived at 10.15 pm. Ethel told the doctor that her husband had been having fits for the past two years but also blamed it on the corned beef that he loved so much. The doctor decided that Arthur had suffered an epileptic fit and dosed him with opium and castor oil.

Arthur settled down for a troubled night but he seemed to improve. In the morning Ethel gave him a cup of warm water. Soon after this he had another attack, which he struggled to survive.

For a while Arthur seemed to recover, but after a few hours he experienced a relapse, had further fits and spasms, then died. His dying words, spoken to his wife, were 'I'm going to die. Don't leave me yet, you have been good to me'. Doctor Smith certified his death due to 'status epilepticus' at 10.40 pm on Friday night. Ethel told her sister-in-law that Major had been taken ill while repairing his bike.

Ethel Major made rather hasty arrangements for a funeral, which she justified on the grounds that the Rector was going away on the Monday. All seemed to be going smoothly until the local coroner received an anonymous letter, with the result that the police arrived at No. 2 just a couple of hours before the funeral was due to start on the Sunday. The interruption of funeral preparations was soon followed by the arrival of a medical team who took control of the corpse. Vital organs were removed and sent for analysis, revealing heavy traces of strychnine.

The letter that triggered these events came, in fact, from Herbert Maltby who lived at No.1. He had two dogs, which Mrs Major notoriously disliked. In his letter he described how Ethel had been seen in the back garden, by another neighbour, Elsie Roberts, scraping a plate of food onto the ground and had

The major family home at Kirkby on Bain

smiled as one of his dogs came up to eat it. This was unusual enough to attract his attention, for she would never have done anything kind to his dogs. Within hours his dog was wretchedly ill so that by eight o'clock that evening 'it was alive but stiff, and with its muscles twitching.' By 9.30 pm it could not open its mouth and it was dead by the morning. As this had happened on the same evening that Major was taken ill, Maltby made a connection and the dog was exhumed on the Saturday, following police orders. A post-mortem revealed that the dog had died from strychnine poisoning.

Meanwhile the police searched Ethel's father's house. Tom Brown, a retired gamekeeper, had strychnine on the premises in a small wooden box, which he kept locked. Back at the council houses, police mentioned to Mrs Major that her husband might have been poisoned and she retorted by saying, 'I never had any strychnine poison.' This was taken to be revealing evidence, for no-one at the time had mentioned the word 'strychnine' to her, but was later ruled out because other people might have mentioned it to her. She told the police that her husband had had spells of dizziness and fainting, but no one else was aware of this.

A search of Mrs Major's property was very productive, however, for a small key was found in her purse, which matched the wooden box at Tom Brown's in which the poison had been kept. Mr Brown said that the key had been 'lost' years earlier, but this was a conclusive connection that Ethel could not escape. Yet even here there is still a mystery – why did she keep such vital evidence?

Ethel Major was arrested on 9th July 1934 in dramatic fashion. When Chief Inspector Young of Scotland Yard arrived at the council houses at five o'clock in the evening, to carry out the arrest, Mrs Major was out visiting her father. Therefore, the police had to stand around for an hour and a half while they waited for her to return. After her arrest, Ethel emerged from the house to be taken into custody, dressed in the black outfit that she was to wear throughout her subsequent public appearances. She was then taken to Horncastle to be charged, before being moved on to Louth, the only available police station with cells for women. She was charged with the murder of her husband at Horncastle magistrates' court the next morning. She was then remanded into custody at Hull prison.

Ethel Major was tried at Lincoln on 29th October. Reports described her as 'a frail, sallow-complexioned woman'. The defence argued that Arthur Major had poisoned himself, following a life of failure. They suggested that the discovery of the secret love letters had been yet another blow and he had descended into alcoholism.

The food arrangements in the Major household proved to be crucial for the prosecution's case. It was shown that Arthur never left his own food in the house when he went out, and that the Major's son had bought the fatal corned beef on his mother's instructions.

As to the vital key, the defence argued that Mrs Major's possession of it *proved* her innocence. Wouldn't she have thrown it away if she were really guilty? They also tried to prove that the love letters had been written by Rose Kettleborough. Ethel's daughter Auriel appeared as a witness, saying that she had seen Rose and Arthur 'making eyes' at each other. 'Attractive, nineteen-year old' Auriel also testified that her father was often drunk and Mrs Major's own father stated that Major was often dizzy. Mrs Kettleborough appeared to deny the accusations of a relationship with Major and that she had written the letters.

Crucially, though, the defence never called Ethel herself as a witness, so her side of the story was never told and she was never directly questioned in court. The jury had little hesitation in finding her guilty of murder, but entered a recommendation of mercy on the grounds that she had led a torrid existence with a drunken and abusive husband. Mr Justice Charles sentenced her to death, observing, 'You have been guilty of one of the cruellest crimes you could have committed.' Mrs Major sobbed and declared herself to be innocent. She then broke down completely and had to be carried from the court.

Ethel's legal team appealed against the death sentence, but this was dismissed. Even the Lord Mayor of Hull tried to get a reprieve, and a Kirkby woman started a petition for mercy, yet it was all in vain.

The night before the execution, Ethel was given a heavy sedative to help her sleep so that she was still only semi-conscious when she went to the scaffold under the supervision of executioner Pierrepoint. There were reports that, at the end, she had expressed her repentance. Her father, Tom Brown, denied this, however, and insisted that she protested her innocence to the end.

The case of Ethel Major attracted the attention of Violet van der Elst. Despite her exotic-sounding name, she was a former scullery maid who had amassed a large fortune from the invention of the first brushless shaving cream, Shavex. She became a tireless campaigner against capital punishment and used the case of Ethel Major in her arguments, publicising details of how Mrs Major's head became detached from her body during the hanging in 1937. Violet bought Harlaxton Hall, a vast decaying mansion near Grantham, and promptly banned all shooting and hunting in its grounds. She died a year after the abolition of capital punishment.

FLYING SAUCER FEVER

———————— ✿ ————————

On 12th August 1954, a 'luminous white disc' was spotted at a height of about 40,000 feet over Gosberton in the Holland fens. The disc moved across the sky quickly, but left no vapour trail and made no noise. This was one of the first of a series of unexplained sightings of strange objects floating in the Lincolnshire skies, which carry on to this day and have fuelled speculation about the possibility of life beyond our own planet.

If it were not for the fact that these sightings continue to occur, it would be easy to dismiss the early reports, such as that at Gosberton, as a phenomenon of their time. Post-war Britain was going through a period of great uncertainty. Communism was a growing threat, a fear matched by the development of atomic missiles and nuclear bombs, and people looked for an escape from the drab reality of their daily lives. One outlet was a fascination for 'sci-fi'. American comic books and cheap B-movies exploited this interest and fostered the view that inter-planetary travel would soon be a possibility. There were those who were eagerly expecting visitors from some distant planet to arrive at any moment and demand to be 'taken to your leader'.

But for the man in Gosberton his experience was very real. His encounter happened in the early evening so it would have been light enough to spot something. Furthermore no one has ever put forward any other interpretation for this or any of the succeeding reports.

It was only a year after the Gosberton incident that *The Echo* received an excited call from farm worker Albert Smith. What

Donald Keyhoe spent his life investigating and writing about 'flying saucers'

he reported set up a chain of other 'sightings' of what became one of the best recorded of the county's UFO encounters.

Smith and his wife had been walking home at about 11.15pm when they were taken aback by a most unusual spectacle drifting in the night sky above them as they neared South Carlton. Firstly, they became aware of a humming noise, 'like a humming top', and then Smith described seeing 'a thing' in the sky. He went on to embellish this further: 'We could see a big saucer-shaped thing with two smaller ones behind it. An orange light came on right on top of the first one. This is no fantastic yarn. The thing was definitely there. It frightened my wife.'

Smith's attempts to hide his own fears behind those of his wife are almost quite touching! Perhaps they were scared they would be snatched away by dwellers from another galaxy to be experimented upon, an understandable paranoia given the fact that the strange saucers hovered menacingly above them before fading away into the clouds.

Smith also claimed that two Americans drove up in a jeep and observed the strange spacecraft before it faded away. Oddly no American names were reported in the press, nor were they interviewed.

The Echo carried the story the next day, though there was some suspicion that the RAF could explain the incident if they chose to do so. They didn't – or couldn't. The nearest airfield was at Scampton, where the authorities stated that all aircraft had returned to base by about 9.30pm, leaving the skies clear for alien visitations.

It is perhaps worthwhile noting at this point that Lincolnshire had more than its fair share of RAF bases. Massive construction projects at airfields like Scampton were underway to ready them for new squadrons of Vulcan bombers, which would have the capacity to drop atomic or nuclear bombs on enemies thousands of miles away. In addition, research into the development of more effective rockets and missiles was taking place and soon supposedly 'secret' missile bases also became a feature of the Lincolnshire landscape.

However, the report in *The Echo* elicited a wealth of calls from other local people who claimed to have heard or seen something the same night as the Smiths. In Saxilby, a woman was on her way to her Women's Institute meeting, when, in her words, she heard 'an unusual chug-chug noise in the sky; it did not sound like an aeroplane to me'. She was unable to actually see anything in conditions of poor visibility, but believed the sound travelled from west to east across Saxilby.

Her story was given further credence by two men who had been sitting indoors in Nettleham when they were disturbed by a 'humming' noise outside, at about 11 o'clock that night. They went out to take a look but were unable to see anything, though the noise continued and was described by them as different from the aeroplane sounds with which they were familiar.

The mystery was perpetuated still further when the next day the paper carried an account of an entirely separate incident described by ex-fighter pilot Neville Berryman of Nettleham Road, Lincoln. It would be hard to find a more sceptical witness than Berryman who told the newspaper categorically that he did not believe in flying saucers. Nonetheless, Berryman was puzzled by what he had seen out of his bedroom window, something that he described as 'a most peculiar thing I can't explain away'.

Berryman may have been a sceptic, but he was certainly a credible witness, mainly due to the high-quality observational skills he would have had to employ during his own RAF days. He described seeing a 'spherical object, golden in colour, like a little sun'. Although it was only in view for 'about two and a half seconds', Berryman confidently reported that it was at a height of about 5,000 feet and travelling at 'a fantastic speed' from north-east to south-west. He heard no sound but estimated it must have been travelling at about 1,500 mph. Berryman said that he had laughed at a Scampton RAF officer who claimed to have seen a flying saucer, although he was unable to offer any alternative explanation as to what he himself had witnessed.

One theory put forward was that it was the flare of a rocket fired from a test base, most likely Faldingworth to the north-east of Lincoln. But, as the rocket would have been heading inland, this seems a highly improbable and dangerous strategy, leaving Berryman's extraordinary experience still unsolved.

Over the succeeding years, occasional sightings have kept the mystery of whether or not we are being watched by aliens very much alive. Experiences such as that recounted by Lance Wingad, who as a schoolboy in 1960 used to go to the brickpits

Were 'gliding' Vulcan bombers responsible for the rash of UFO sightings in Lincolnshire? (Lincolnshire Echo)

in Bracebridge, just south of Lincoln, to do a spot of fishing. Going down into the brickpits was rather like going down into another world. Once at the bottom you were isolated from the rest of civilisation, surrounded by the steep sides of the pit and a patch of sky above. Chancing to glance up into the sky during one of these expeditions, Lance saw what he describes as 'a shape like a rugby ball, except it was silver'. The object appeared to hover more or less motionless in the atmosphere above, before moving northwards.

Lance, who later became an engineer, was hugely impressed with the way the craft appeared to gather speed with great power and yet made no sound whatsoever. Shortly afterwards it returned from the north to hover in the sky over Bracebridge once again, before accelerating away at great speed towards the south. Lance was not alone and his friends corroborated his story. 'I told my parents,' he said, 'because we were frightened.'

To this day Lance is convinced that he had an eerie encounter with a UFO, and he is also in no doubt about its mission. 'They had come to observe our own primitive flying machines,' he reveals, 'because the craft showed obvious interest in the RAF stations at Waddington and Scampton.'

Lance's explanation could well be supported by another sighting two years later on 12th December 1962 when Peter Bolton saw an 'object' over RAF Coningsby. Rationalists must have thought it was quite a likely place to see a flying object, although they may not have been quite so dismissive if they had witnessed what Bolton claimed was anything but a normal aircraft.

Man's obsession with the possibility of encounters with extra terrestrials carried on into the 1970s, beginning with the mysterious disappearance of an American pilot thought by some to have been kidnapped by aliens (see chapter 5). It continued with other strange descriptions of peculiar airborne craft shimmering in the Lincolnshire skies. Gary Heseltine was a schoolboy in 1975, enjoying an evening walk along a footpath near his school in Scunthorpe, accompanied by a young lady. Their stroll was abruptly interrupted by a sudden blinding flash of a brilliant white light, which zoomed across them from right to left. The couple watched in astonishment as it passed slowly over the houses, seeming to cut off all electrical power in its wake and plunging unsuspecting householders into darkness. Gary reached his own home just as the light was passing over, and told his parents that the power was about to go off, which it did, remaining 'out' for half an hour.

It was a truly strange and inexplicable incident, which left a lasting impression on the young Gary Heseltine. When he later became a policeman, so vivid was his encounter with another world that Gary set up a website to record incidents passed on by fellow police officers who reported seeing UFOs.

In March 1976 a single witness was stunned by what appeared above him near Ulceby Cross in north Lincolnshire in what was truly a 'close' encounter. He described seeing a huge craft, around 45 feet across, and therefore much bigger than the Vulcan bombers. Although similar in shape, this craft appeared 'perfectly triangular' unlike the Vulcan, which is dominated by its delta-wing. It also seemed to be solid, as if made of a single piece of metal. It passed frighteningly close over the witness's head, at a height of about 50 feet, and was travelling slowly, he estimated somewhere between 15 and 40 mph, as if on reconnaissance. Two dazzling lights at the very front of the craft beamed down at 90° angles, making it difficult to see any detail, but from underneath the vessel there seemed to come a curious bluish glow.

There are those determined not to believe there could be any mystery about this truly weird experience and theories have been put forward about 'lighter than air military craft'. But there is no evidence to support this and so the speculation continues.

For UFO enthusiasts the belief that this was probably a ship from outer space is backed up by a startling story from

Kuybyshev, part of the old Soviet Union, nearly 20 years later. In 1990, a similar but smaller object was spotted and landed near a military tracking station. Furthermore two sentries disappeared for two hours. When they reappeared, they had no memory of where they had been and curiously, time had evidently stood still for them because both their watches were two hours slow!

More recently, a well-reported incident caused confusion to the police, coastguards and RAF over Lincolnshire and Norfolk in 1996. At three o'clock one October morning, police at Skegness saw a strange red and green rotating light. This was confirmed by a Conocoast oil tanker out at sea. It was at first believed to be an aircraft, but the fact that it remained stationary for four hours negated this view. Just after four o'clock it was reported to be visible at Boston, but could still be seen by the tanker, which described the lights as 'flashing red, green, blue and white'. At 05.17am, Boston police stated, 'we can still see the light ... just a bright light'.

The sighting was relayed to the coastguard and also to the RAF. The lights were tracked by RAF Neatishead in Norfolk and on the radar at RAF Waddington. A radar trace was still apparent after eleven o'clock in the morning.

Rumours soon started to spread that the police and the RAF were trying to track a UFO, sparking interest from both journalists and the public. Skegness police issued a statement to say: 'We had calls overnight that suggested there was a large bright object suspended over the coast. In the past, sightings like this have been either a plane or a weather balloon.' The *Evening News* reported that two large objects had been seen hovering at a height of about a mile over the Wash and had also shown up on radar screens. The interest generated further reports, for instance a Norwich postman recounted how he had seen a 'star-like object' flying very fast across the sky.

Such was the speculation that the Ministry of Defence was forced to respond. They suggested that the Boston Stump had in fact caused the radar 'blip' and that the coloured lights were actually a phenomenon created by stars. UFO experts greeted this interpretation with derision, whilst it became of some concern to the public that RAF radar technicians could confuse a church tower with a craft in the sky! Ultimately it seems that RAF investigators were at a complete loss to explain away the incident, although those who don't want to believe in life beyond earth hold onto the theory that the coloured lights could have been caused by an electrical storm over the Wash.

So what did this object with the flashing lights look like? Many saw it, but few agreed. Three different descriptions include that it looked like a Farley's Rusk with two bites out of it, that it resembled the Batman symbol, and that it was like an axe-head. The fact remains that we will probably never know what had been hovering over the shoreline that night.

For UFO investigators the 'truth is definitely out there' but even they can get a little wary of sighting frenzy such as that generated in Grimsby in April 2000. On this occasion the papers were accused of playing on local people's fears and imaginations in order to sell more copies. As with many unexplained occurences, once one person's version has been published many more come forward with their experiences, none of which have been disproved.

The Grimsby incident started with the story of a lady from Tetney who claimed to have had a series of 'encounters'. One morning, she opened the door into one of her rooms and found two 'beings' there with a man on a table. Beyond that she didn't elaborate, as she was concerned for her welfare. She had already lost two cats and had recently had her pony put down, all of which she felt had some sinister overtone. Her story generated a response from a man who had been washing his car in Willingham Street with his niece when a white object had appeared in the sky above them, where it stayed for about four minutes before drifting away into the heavens.

Two local women also sent in information. A Humberston woman saw a silver cigar-shaped object surrounded by a pink glow in Waltham. It was visible for five or six minutes and made no sound. A Cleethorpes woman saw a round, bright light on 24th March. She was getting the washing in at the time, and saw a 'big round gold shining light' over the Humber estuary. She was convinced it wasn't a plane because it was travelling much too fast as it climbed higher in the sky over Spurn Head and disappeared. A schoolboy also came forward saying he had seen something similar at about the same time.

Although Grimsby may not be the most obvious place for aliens to target when visiting earth, it seems that the Lincolnshire coast has been at the centre of a number of strange and inexplicable sightings of unfamiliar objects in the sky. In the same year as the Grimsby cases, two other stories occurred further along the coast. In the first, a couple in a car travelling on the Boston road, twelve miles south of Skegness, saw a bright flashing light in the eastern sky, three miles out at sea. They then saw what they identified as two helicopters come clattering across and converge on the bright light. What happened to them? In the other case, another couple reported seeing a very large, noisy, slow-moving craft, which made the ground vibrate. It is one of the few reports claiming that the alien spaceship was especially noisy.

The one common element in all these incidents is that none of them have been fully explained. People can be cynical about flashing lights and odd shapes in the sky, laughing them off as the workings of vivid imaginations, but how do they know that somewhere in space another civilisation isn't trying to come up with a rational explanation for the odd glimpse of our own satellite stations or space rockets? For many people it is a strongly held belief, and judging by the various stories from Lincolnshire a perfectly plausible one, that we are definitely *not* alone.

THE DOG WHO SHOT
A FARMER

Lt-Col Halland, Chief Constable of Lincolnshire was perplexed by the latest sensational killing, which had shocked the county in December 1931. A young man, James Kitchen, had been shot dead at point-blank range in broad daylight at a farm in Gedney Marsh, and the best his officers could come up with was that the murderer was the dead man's dog!

Halland knew he had no choice but to ring for assistance from London. Like all self-respecting provincial policemen, he hated to do this, but he badly needed the expert help of Professor Sir Bernard Spilsbury. As he asked his secretary to put a call through to London, he must have wondered how Spilsbury would react when he told him who the local officers had identified as the chief suspect.

His phone rang, and Spilsbury's clipped Home Counties accent greeted him cordially. 'Halland!' he said, 'what's this about a killing in the Fens?' One can imagine Halland's discomfort as he explained to the scientist that the chief suspect in the case of a man shot at point blank range with a shotgun was a dog.

It seems, however, that this was enough to capture Spilsbury's interest. It was certainly an unusual case, even if unlikely to turn out to be premeditated murder. So Spilsbury was soon in the Fens, driving past Holbeach and out to Brook House Farm in Gedney Marsh, the scene of the crime. On his arrival, he examined the scene of James Kitchen's death at the door of a barn. He posed for photographs in the local papers, and took away a double-barrelled shotgun, which had been identified as the 'murder weapon'.

Halland must have realised that the case had the potential to be an embarrassment to his force, especially when the story hit the evening papers on Friday, 4th December. The Fens was an area where most men kept a loaded shotgun and a dog with them at all times, for you never knew when a nice plump duck was likely to fly over head. Guns went off frequently, even by accident, but no one had ever heard of a dog managing to set off a shotgun. The day after the death, local police attempted to stage a torchlight reconstruction of events at the barn door, which attracted a crowd of fascinated locals. They all wanted to see how the police were going to get a dog to repeat its cunning trick of shooting a man when he wasn't looking.

James Kitchen was found shot outside this barn in Gedney Marsh (Lincolnshire Echo)

But there was also a much darker undercurrent of feeling about how the police were handling the case. Local rumour said that the real murderer was actually James's father George, who just happened to be a retired Metropolitan police constable. It looked suspiciously like the police were protecting one of their own.

George Kitchen had moved to the Fens after retiring from the police force and earned his keep with a spot of farming. Lacking sufficient capital to buy a place of his own, he rented Brook House Farm from Holland County Council in partnership with his two sons, James and William. In 1931 George was 63 and James was 36, although he was still a bachelor and lived at home.

According to George, both he and James had gone out as usual on that Friday morning, the father slightly ahead of the son. It was 200 yards from the farmhouse to the barn and James was carrying his loaded shotgun as usual. George walked on into the yard, but James stopped to release his dog from the outhouse where it kept watch. He then propped his shotgun up against the wall of the meal house so that he could clean a shovel in a puddle. It was at that moment that the old man said he heard an 'explosion'. He rushed across to find his son on the floor, blasted by the shotgun, and the dog rushing around. He ran to get help from three men in a field nearby and together they carried James into the barn, where he died shortly afterwards.

George insisted from the start that the death of his son was a bizarre accident, but his protestations did nothing to calm the atmosphere in the fenland settlements. Some scoffed openly at the idea that a dog could cause a gun to go off and shoot its master, while others spread rumours about a dangerous maniac on the loose. It was reported that the inhabitants of Gedney Marsh were convinced the murderer was still around, and children were kept out of school.

One of the strangest inquests ever held in Lincolnshire took place in the farmhouse where the Kitchen family lived. A crowd

George Kitchen whose son James was thought to have been shot by his dog (Lincolnshire Echo)

of solemn faces filled the house, in stark contrast to the Christmas decorations adorning the walls. Firstly, the coroner asked for William Kitchen, brother of the deceased to give evidence as to his identity – which he quickly did. Then he blurted out, 'I cannot tell you anything about the tragedy,' before the coroner cautioned him to remain silent.

The police let it be known that Spilsbury was conducting experiments with the flight of a bullet to see if the dog story could be correct. But at the inquest much excitement was caused when it was reported that Spilsbury was not yet ready to present his findings. Whilst people whispered about intensive new police enquiries, George Kitchen got up to state his own views to the coroner.

'Jimmy was never murdered,' he said, trying to scotch the maniac on the loose theory. 'He didn't harm anybody and nobody would harm him. My son has no enemies as far as I know.' But the tide of rumours was gathering strength. People were saying that the old man was suspiciously close when the shotgun went off. George reported, however, that his son had left the gun cocked ready to fire in case of geese. Did the father have a reason to shoot his son? Everyone knew that relations between them had sometimes been bad and that the previous year the old man had been seen chasing his son with a rifle and a gun. It was also common knowledge that his behaviour had been so bad that his wife and sons had barred him from sleeping in his own home. The inquest was adjourned, pending further reports.

The pressure of rumour and innuendo had its effect on the family. The day after the inquest was adjourned the tension was high while everyone waited to hear what Spilsbury's investigations uncovered. That night Mrs Kitchen, mother of the dead man, finally cracked under the stress, vanishing from her house into the darkness of the Fenland winter. Soon there were torchlights flickering all over the marshes as people searched the dykes fearing that she might have drowned herself. Eventually Mrs Kitchen was found, bewildered but safe, several miles away.

Meanwhile, further credence was added to the accident theory from elsewhere in Lincolnshire when, just before Christmas, a farm labourer was shot by his own gun when he stumbled while walking.

When Spilsbury finally reported his conclusions to Lincolnshire police, he offered the conclusion that the gun had been fired from at least three feet away and, crucially, that it had been pointing downwards due to the angle of entry into the body. It must, therefore, have been in the hands of someone who took deliberate shot and could not have been fired from its position against the wall or on the ground, which were the only possible places from which the dog could have activated the trigger.

The police, meanwhile, had compiled plenty of other information about George Kitchen's bad temper and armed with the eminent professor's views, they finally acted. George Kitchen was arrested at the farm on 12th January 1932. Sergeant Lown took him into custody in front of Mrs Kitchen, who said, 'I will stake my life he didn't do it,' before fainting. The suspect was taken away to the cells at Spalding.

The arrest of Kitchen at last put a stop to the ridicule to which the police had been subjected. The case was scheduled to be heard at the Old Bailey in April and queues of people over sixty yards long waited for entry to the court. The prosecution case, argued by J. Eales KC, was that the gun must have been pointing downwards and that it must therefore have been murder. Eales elaborated his view, explaining that the men in the fields had seen George Kitchen with a gun before the shot was heard, and also that he had a motive – the old man was known to be bad-tempered, and had been heard threatening his son. The arguments had gone on for years, and Eales was able to call a witness who had heard George threaten to shoot and cripple his son.

There followed a setback for the prosecution case, however, when sketches of the murder scene, presented by PC Robinson, were compared with photographs of the same place. There were a number of differences and therefore, it was insinuated, Robinson's evidence could not be trusted at all. Then came the moment everyone was waiting for. Prince, the black retriever, was brought into court and placed on the solicitor's table. He remained a mute witness though, taking no sides, but appearing to listen patiently to a detailed discussion as to whether a tab on his collar could have caught in the gun. The victim's brother, William Kitchen, demonstrated to the court how the dog's collar was tied.

After the dog was removed William was required to give evidence. Watching journalists detected some bad feeling between the son in the witness box and the father in the dock for it was noticed that there was a quick glance between father and son and that their eyes met only once during the long examination. Then came Thomas Armes of Wisbech, the owner of the gun, and a friend of the dead man; he reported the quarrels and threats that he had heard.

The most dramatic appearance was that of Spilsbury. Firstly the scientist gave evidence about the distance from which the gun was fired and the direction from which the shot entered the body. But under cross-examination it became rapidly clear that Spilsbury had only a limited idea of what had really happened and the prosecution case began to unravel. He was certain about the angle of shot but, the defence asked, did he know the position of the victim at the time the shot was fired? Was James Kitchen standing up, bending over, or lying down? Spilsbury had to admit that he did not know exactly how the wound was inflicted, whether by dog or man, and the judge decided to intervene. He stopped the trial.

George Kitchen stepped from the Old Bailey a free man. Though he appeared to have the motive and the attitude to commit murder, nobody could be certain beyond reasonable doubt. After the trial, he made a statement to the press, declaring his innocence:

'It has been a great strain, but I felt sure I should get off. I am very glad it is all over. I am going back to Lincolnshire for a rest, and I don't know what I am going to do in the future.'

Although George was cleared of murder, he never really gained true liberty. His family had buckled under the strain and his reputation was clearly damaged by the allegations. The collapse of the case had left a bad feeling and the Fenland community closed ranks against him. Eventually, George, was forced to make a new beginning elsewhere.

The only one to come out unscathed from the whole messy business was Prince, who was able to live out the rest of his days in peace and probably recalled nothing of the death of his master and his day in court.

LOVE'S BITTER HARVEST

—❀—

Between 1914 and 1918 the men of Lincolnshire, like all young men across the country, went off to fight in the Great War. Many of them never returned. Of those that did, a considerable number carried physical and mental scars, which would affect the rest of their lives. In those days, people were better able to understand those who were physically disabled, rather than those carrying the emotional scars, which meant they could no longer handle the small ups and downs of normal life. Some found it hard to settle to a job, while others sought to rekindle relationships from before the War, although still troubled by dark memories.

It was this mental trauma that lead to three Lincolnshire ex-soldiers committing acts of murder which saw two of them ending up on the gallows. Thus the War inadvertently claimed two further victims.

George Rowland had all the qualifications for a war hero. He had joined the Army at the start of the conflict and had spent four years fighting. He was wounded three times, but found it difficult to recount his experiences.

George returned to his home in Grantham aged 29, determined to get his life back to normal. No doubt he had in mind to find a girl and settle down. He soon became a familiar sight around the villages north of Grantham, especially when he met up with 19-year-old Florence Jackson, a pretty young domestic servant from Welbourn. Florence knew nothing of the realities of war and, to George, seemed to offer the hope of a completely new start. That she was good-looking must have been an added bonus.

After 'keeping company' for some time, the couple went to the Caythorpe Feast one evening and this led to disaster. Rowland was ten years older than the girl, but his experiences during the War made him seem much older still. His memories made him serious and withdrawn at times, whereas Florence was still growing up in a world of giggling young girls and boys barely out of their short trousers who liked 'a lark'. At the feast, Florence was determined to have fun and became, it seems, a little flirtatious as well. Rowland could not control his jealousy when his young lady went in the swing boats with a friend of his. He became emotional and fiercely argumentative about Florence's behaviour. After laying into his friend with a few choice words, Rowland turned back to Florence and began to drag out other things that he had heard about her unseemly behaviour. There was, he said, a good story about a dashing young sergeant from the Royal Flying Corps who had come calling for Florence. He went on to allege that Florence had 'been with' the sergeant, words that would have carried a moral stigma in 1919. Perhaps Florence was already tiring of Rowland; the novelty of being admired by an older man would soon have palled, especially when he was so possessive and prone to violent mood swings.

Rowland insisted that Florence was still 'his girl' though, and therefore had the proprietorial responsibility of seeing her home. Just after ten that night, the couple set off to Fulbeck along an 'occupation road' to a place known as Gascoign's Gate. This was a rough farm track, and not the 'Cliff Road', the usual route between the villages. It may have been what is now a footpath running from near Caythorpe Hall further west past some woods.

Just after 10 o'clock another man, Richard Snelson, took this route home as well and, as far as we know, he was unaccompanied. At about 10.30pm he came upon the terrifying scene of a blood-soaked man rearing up in front of him. It was Rowland and he was wounded and bleeding.

Rowland told him, 'There has been a nasty accident. A girl has tried to cut my throat and now she has cut her own.' The scene must have shocked Snelson, for Rowland was indeed bleeding heavily around the throat and nearby was the prostrate and bloody form of Florence Jackson.

Snelson examined the body to confirm that she was dead and observed cuts to the throat and an open razor in her hand.

Rowland made feeble attempts to support his story of Florence as the aggressor. Having told Snelson that the girl had attacked him, however, he later told Florence's sister, 'I have killed your Flo.' The simple-minded Rowland did not have the mental agility to sustain a convincing explanation.

Rowland was arrested and put on trial at Lincoln. There Dr Alfred Ewan of the Kesteven County Asylum appeared to give evidence as to whether Rowland was fit to stand trial, and clearly stated a negative view. The ex-soldier could not read or write, and had a mental age of about 12, the doctor told the jury. His evidence was, however, disregarded and the trial continued. In fact further evidence about Rowland's mental state did play a major part in the proceedings. When his father appeared, Mr Rowland explained that his son had been wounded three times, and also testified that he had been gassed. His behaviour was 'disturbed', he said, and he described how George would shout out at night, 'Jerry's over the top! They're coming!'

There was little doubt about Rowland having murdered Florence Jackson. The feeble attempt to suggest that she had slashed at his throat before cutting her own was shown to be hopeless. Apart from anything else, the angle of the cuts to the girl's throat meant that they could not have been self-inflicted. But Rowland escaped the gallows, owing to his disturbed mental state, and his sentence was commuted to penal servitude for life.

Two other war veterans who escaped the Germans were not so fortunate. 13th December 1922 was a sad and unusual day in the history of Lincolnshire crime, for both men were executed in Lincoln and for very similar murders.

The killers were fairly young men who had taken the lives of younger women with whom they were romantically obsessed. The murders were also significant in being the second and third murders in Lincoln to have been committed by veterans of the Great War. One of the issues must be whether the experiences of the trenches affected these young men, who might otherwise never have even considered carrying out such a dreadful crime.

The first victim was the 18 year old daughter of a widowed woman. On 23rd September 1922 life was going well for Mrs d'Arcy, the licensee of the *White Horse* in Market Deeping. She was celebrating her imminent wedding to a Mr Kitchener of Tallington which was to take place on 25th September and the recent marriage of her daughter Ivy, which had occurred on 20th September. In the private rooms of the *White Horse*, Mrs d'Arcy had laid out her wedding gifts for her daughter and others to look at, when she noticed a farm manager named Frank Fowler standing at the door. He was the *last* person she wanted to see; a sullen and morose character who had walked out with her daughter for a while and who had been *very* difficult to get rid of. She knew he would cause trouble, because he always did, but she could never have anticipated the terrible turn of events about to unfold.

Without a word, Fowler suddenly drew out a shotgun and opened fire into the room. He then calmly paused to reload. Seeing him about to fire again, Mrs d'Arcy lunged forwards to knock the shotgun barrel around so the second shot went harmlessly through the pub window. Customers from the bar came running at the sound of the gunfire, but they were too slow to catch Fowler who disappeared into the town. They were also too late to save Ivy, who, after three days of marriage to George Prentice, had been fatally hit by the first shot from Fowler's gun.

One would have expected that the *White Horse* would at least have been closed for the rest of the day, but that evening it was business as usual as customers enjoyed their drinks in the bar. No doubt the main topic of conversation was the day's shocking events. In the midst of all this in walked Fowler and calmly bought a round of drinks.

Most of the customers were too astonished by this show of brazen gall to speak to him, but when Ivy's sister discovered he was present she went straight up to speak to him.

'You have shot my sister,' she said outright.

'Yes,' he replied, 'and I meant the other for your mother.'

Not surprisingly, he was soon deprived of the freedom to drink in the *White Horse* and locked up in the cells on a charge of murder and attempted murder.

With such clear evidence and many witnesses, there was little doubt of Fowler's guilt although some evidence of mental problems did emerge. The court was told that Ivy had been 'a pretty girl with a smile and a joke for everyone'. Clearly she loved the sociable life at the hotel, whereas Fowler lived on a farm out at Langtoft and was 'of a somewhat sullen and morose disposition.'

Fowler's father had been 'notoriously mentally deficient', but his son had found work with an aunt until joining the army and going off to fight in the Great War. His aunt gave evidence that, after being demobbed, he had been 'queer in his ways'. She described how he was prone to sudden mood swings, switching from swearing at her to singing hymns. He had also complained of being followed or watched. The aunt also had to tell the court that he had twice threatened to cut her throat. There was great confusion about what Fowler himself had said about the crime, one of his most mysterious utterances being 'Teasdale knows something about this.' Teasdale was a man from Towngate who used to go to the *White Horse*, but no one could see any connection between him and what had happened.

With modern understanding we could probably deduce that Fowler was suffering some form of mental illness, perhaps induced by the stresses of war. Young Ivy, though, had had little sympathy for his troubled past. She had become more interested in a young hairdresser named George Prentice. Fowler had been one of Prentice's customers until he discovered that he was a rival in love. Clearly Fowler had decided that if he could not have Ivy then Prentice should not have her either.

Fowler went to his death alongside George Robinson of Dorrington. Robinson had murdered 18 year-old Frances Pacey at Dorrington. He was 27 years of age, and described as 'a medium-sized, fresh-complexioned, good-looking young man'. Nonetheless he had also been to War and in peacetime was struggling to put his life back together. He began walking out with Frances early in 1922, and she, like the other victims in this chapter, was several years younger than her suitor. Again the relationship did not develop happily, and on April 9th she told him that it was over. Robinson was plunged into despair, telling his lost-love that all he could think of doing now was to go away and cut his own throat.

Instead of carrying out his threat, Robinson pursued Frances, hoping that she could be persuaded to renew their attachment. She was not interested, however, and his mood seems to have become darker over the summer months. He was madly jealous and did not even like Frances to talk to other girls. Struck down by depression, Robinson gave up his job, and spent many days hanging around at home or trying to catch a glimpse of Frances.

Early on 5th September, Frances' mother went out and left the girl alone in their home, even though Robinson was seen to have been hanging around. When she had gone, Robinson went to the house and was either admitted, or simply let himself in, we will never know. A few minutes later, Frances came rushing out of the house bleeding from a cut to the throat. She ran to a neighbour's house in her nightgown, screaming, 'Oh! I'm done for!' Attempts were made to help her and the nearest doctor was summoned. When Dr Woods of

Ruskington arrived he found Frances on the floor in her nightdress, covered with blood but still alive.

The doctor was about to leave, with his patient in his car, when he was intercepted by a group of people, who told him of another emergency. Robinson had been seen going back to his own house 'looking wild' and with blood marks across his chest. When people rushed to his house, it was found that he had attempted to cut his own throat and still had the razor he had used in his pocket.

The doctor, however, found Robinson in bed, 'looking remarkably well', but with a three inch long gash in his throat. Robinson's sister gave evidence that her brother had come home blood-spattered, but the good doctor reported only that there was 'a little' blood on the floor. In fact the sister had made a good effort to hide the evidence of his guilt. She had collected together his blood-spattered clothes and taken them down to a pond to wash, since the cottage had no water supply of its own. The doctor decided that Robinson also needed hospital treatment so, being short of emergency transport, he put the assailant in the same car as the victim for the trip to Lincoln Hospital!

When Frances died that afternoon, it became a murder investigation, albeit one that involved little mystery to tax the ingenuity of the police. Conclusive proof was provided when it was revealed that a small piece of steel found in Frances Pacey's neck wound exactly matched a piece missing from the razor blade found in Robinson's coat pocket. Robinson's cap was found in the dead girl's bedroom and, even though his sister had washed all his clothes, a spot of blood was found on his waistcoat.

In his defence, it was pointed out that Robinson had served in France and had been thrown off a mule, injuring his head. The inference being that the incident may have caused a mental unbalance. Although there was much discussion of his possibly suffering from 'melancholia', Robinson was found guilty of murder with no allowance for mental health problems.

Robinson and Prentice were put in separate 'Condemned Cells' only 17 ft from the scaffold in Lincoln Prison. They were executed on a double scaffold on 13 December 1922.

THE MYSTERIOUS BIG CATS
OF LINCOLNSHIRE

---- ❁ ----

One night in March 2003, Rachel Wydrzynska was driving along Tillbridge Lane north of Lincoln. It was half-past ten and the road was fairly quiet. Rachel was near the county showground when she was astonished to see a large creature 'pounce off' into the darkness.

'It was definitely a large cat-like creature,' she said, clearly aware that some people would say she was seeing things. 'It was the size of a largish dog but definitely moved like a cat with one bound from one side of the road to the other. It was grey, and another thing that struck me was the speed with which it moved. I can't remember seeing a tail at the time but at one point it was only ten metres from the front of my bonnet.'

This might seem easier to believe if it was an account from 100 or more years ago, given by a farmer on his way home from market. But Rachel's story is very much in the present, as are all the sightings mentioned in this chapter.

One of the surprising things about Rachel's case is that she had never heard of there being big cats in Lincolnshire, even though there had been many reported encounters. 'I'd never heard of the Lincoln Lynx,' she said, 'and it was only when I got back home and told people about my sighting that they, in turn, told me about this creature.' Rachel referred to one lynx, but when we add the stories all together it becomes difficult to avoid the conclusion that there may be rather more than just a single creature out there, patrolling the woods and lanes by night.

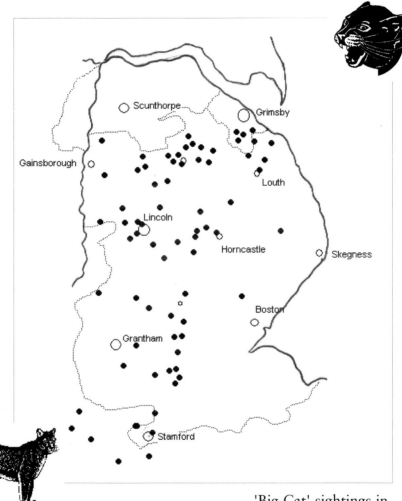

'Big Cat' sightings in
Lincolnshire, 1993–2003

One area with plenty of reported sightings is around Market Rasen, where huge footprints were found in Willingham Woods in August 1994. But one of the first actual appearances of the so-called 'Wolds Panther' was at Market Rasen in April 1995, a town better-known for proud racehorses than skulking cats. One evening Anna Troughton and her son were in Gallamore Lane industrial estate when she saw a large cat from a distance of about six feet. It was about two and a half feet high, and quite calm. 'It was not at all frightened of my son,' she said, 'It just turned to look at him, lifted its top lip and snarled, and then just ambled away.' She was so astonished at what she had seen that she brought her family back the next evening to see if it would return to the same spot. This time they all saw it. A few days later the Market Rasen police reported that a large, feral tomcat was active in the area, but the Troughton family poured scorn on this explanation. They were convinced that they had seen something a lot bigger than any tomcat.

Soon afterwards, the Wolds Panther was seen again, but this time out in the country between Faldingworth and Snarford crossroads. A Mrs Rayland reported a detailed description of the beast, which sounded rather frightening: 'It was very very large and very shiny. It was taller than a fully-grown Labrador and much longer. From the movement of its body you could tell it was cat-like, it sort of lopes along.' Over the next few months and years, the creature (or its relatives) put in a number of appearances in the district. In October 1995 it appeared near Normanby Cliff, then in January 1996 it jumped out at Edward Whitney as he drove along a forest track near Tealby. Whitney, maintaining the tradition of dog-comparisons, said that it was of similar size to an alsatian. Later that year a woman at Kingerby said she saw a beast the size of an alsatian looking in the windows of her house and large cat-like prints were found in a garden at Osgodby.

There was then a period of quiet until a clutch of sightings at the end of 1997, when an animal was seen during November in

Mill Road, Market Rasen and at Middle Rasen playing fields. A week later it turned up at Walesby caravan park. After this the animal lay low until it was seen at the Willingham Woods picnic site and then again in Gallamore Lane in the late summer of 1998.

Then the Wolds Panther vanished from sight for four years, until reappearing to create surprise if not fear in April 2003. Christine Tye of Ludford was able to report that the creature was four times bigger than a normal cat, with a grey face and a long black tale. She thought it was like a puma, so a re-naming seemed to be required.

Perhaps the Wolds Panther had a smaller relative operating further south for in October 1996 there were reports of a creature at Stenigot and Asterby which was only eighteen inches high although over three feet long.

In fact the Wolds Panther, or puma, was hardly alone in Lincolnshire by this time. Every area of the county now seemed to have its own 'big cat' stories, in which pumas, panthers, lynxes and all other cat-like creatures except for lions and tigers seem to be implicated. If the local press is to be believed, it is a veritable jungle out there, with wild cats of all descriptions each patrolling their territory by day and night. This has led to some competition between newspapers to adopt their own animals, which they usually do by trying to give them a geographically specific name. The first naming of a beast seems to have been in 1993 after Alan Ellis spotted a large cat near Caenby Corner. This was dubbed 'the Lindsey Leopard' by the *Echo*, although there is no evidence of it having really been a leopard. Thus the *Market Rasen Mail* has the 'Wolds Panther', but this is quite possibly the same animal as the one reported in the *Lincolnshire Echo* in March 2003, spotted in Tillbridge Lane by Rachel Wydrzynka and looking the size of 'a largish dog'. The cats, however, seem inclined to wander all over the place, belying the specific town or village labels the papers bestow upon them.

The name 'Lindsey Leopard' (which would have been a really serious cause for concern!) faded eventually, although the sightings did not. Instead it became known as the 'Lindsey Lynx' or 'Lincolnshire Lynx'. One of the most extraordinary appearances was in April 1995, when a motorist spotted a big cat in the woods of Hartsholme Country Park alongside the road at up to 30mph. He described it as over four feet long and black or dark grey in colour. During the same month it was seen lying down near Burton Road and at the old RAF station at Skellingthorpe.

Sightings around Lincoln took place regularly during the summer of 1995. Then there was a long gap until a large cat was spotted in a Lincoln garden in May 1996. This was clearly a cat that was not afraid of human contact, and seems to have been partial to hanging around the backs of houses.

In October 1997 a woman in Oak Avenue, Dunholme, saw one resting on a tree branch for fully 45 minutes and said that it was three feet long. But there was also more worrying evidence that the animals were prepared to attack larger farm creatures. In October 1998 three sheep were attacked near Baumber and when two lambs were savaged at Hemingby in the Wolds during December 1998 the incident was linked to the activities of the lynx. Nearer to someone's actual home, a brown or sandy-coloured creature three times the size of a normal cat was blamed for an attack on a rabbit hutch at Doddington Park, where the mesh was ripped open and two rabbits taken.

Some of the greatest interest has been attached to the reports of big cats actually venturing into the boundaries of the city of Lincoln. In the millennium year, Mrs Flear-Charlton was going out to exercise her daschunds in Higson Road. 'Halfway down the steps we saw a huge black thing. We thought it was a panther,' she said. When the creature turned round to look at her, Mrs Flear-Charlton's first concern was for the safety of her dogs – 'I thought it might eat them,' she said. But fortunately

A police officer poses with plaster casts of giant paw prints, taken from a scene near Gainsborough (The Lincolnshire Echo)

the panther was not interested in a diet of sausage dogs and ambled away.

A rather more fanciful name, 'the Fiskerton Phantom', was used to identify a creature that was spotted in the area east of Lincoln. This attracted attention in October 1997 after scaring children around the area of the Tyrwhitt Arms at Short Ferry. The animal was also supposedly adept at crossing the river and was reported to have reached Potterhanworth and Heighington as well.

In the south of the county, the *Stamford Mercury* reports that the 'Rutland Panther' has been seen over 300 times, and in four different counties. But it has also reported the activities of the

'Bourne Beast' without having any certainty that they are different animals. The Bourne Beast has been especially active recently, having been seen at Dyke, Pointon, Rippingale, Morton, Edenham and Stainfield. Some children in Dyke saw it in 2002 and again in February 2003. When they returned to the same spot the next day, they found large paw prints and a savaged fox. Jacqui Meech of nearby Morton reported having seen a large cat near her house and the following day chickens were found dead at Hanthorpe, just a mile to the west. Actually, sightings of a wild cat in this area go back to two appearances near Aslackby in 1993.

Also keen to get in on the excitement was the *Sleaford Standard*. In November 2001 it reported that a big cat had been seen on the B1394 near Swaton and then in August 2002 one was seen in fields near Ruskington. This animal soon gained confidence, for in September it was seen padding along Parkfield Road in the middle of the village at half past midnight. Could this have been the Bourne Beast?

There have also been a number sightings around Gainsborough, including the one by Rachel Wydrsynska in Tillbridge Lane. One of these sightings, in August 1998, led to some of the best evidence available when plaster casts of paw prints in a farmyard, were taken by the police. These were seen by RSPCA inspector Steve Foster who identified them as puma or lynx prints. They were said to be conclusive evidence that the big cats really did exist. In January 1999 large paw prints, purportedly those of a puma, were again seen near Gainsborough. South of Gainsborough, in Laughton Forest, Chris Till was surprised to find more in the woods than he had expected. He had a close encounter with a big cat while walking his dog in July 2002:

'We had walked about 100 metres down the track when what I think was a cougar walked across my path. It was about 15 metres away, light brown, and was a little over a metre long. I was not scared at all, I was just intrigued by what I had seen.'

Mr Till, who was a chef in the Royal Navy, said that he tried to follow the big cat but it vanished.

Sightings in the Wolds, south and west of Grimsby, have been assiduously reported in the *Grimsby Evening Telegraph*. There were a number of sightings south of Grimsby in 1995, culminating in the discovery of nine dead rabbits at Tetney. A month later the residents of Marshchapel were apparently terrified by the night-time cries of a large cat. There was a rash of activity early in 1998 when three witnesses in different places reported similar descriptions around Holton-le-Clay and Tetney. The animal was described as jet black with a long tail and distinctive movement so it was claimed to be a puma.

On 19 October 1998 a big cat was spotted near Normanby Top and in October 2000, a 'beast' was seen to cross Ludborough bypass in front of a car at 6.10 pm. It was still light, so a good description of an animal about five feet long and two and a half feet high was given.

In October 2003, the Lincolnshire 'big cat' hit the headlines again when Mr and Mrs Sandy Richardson from the village of Hemingby claimed to have videoed a large animal in their garden. Mr Richardson saw a big black cat inside an old caravan in his garden. 'It had large yellow eyes, they were so bright it looked like a light shining from behind them', he said. The sighting attracted much attention, and animal hairs were analysed by an American laboratory, which concluded that they were from a leopard.

A large black cat was sighted in Horsington in February 2004 by retired banker Bernard O'Halloran, who ran out of his house for a better look before remembering that it might be dangerous. Then, on 12th April 2004, between Baumber and Wragby, a driver saw a creature which he described a large black cat, the size of a labrador.

So where have all these big cats come from? The most likely explanation seems to be that they are the result of the Dangerous Wild Animals Act of 1976. This new law imposed strict controls on the types of animals that could be kept in a domestic setting and meant that licences were required. As a result a number of 'exotic pets' became illegal unless kept under strictly regulated conditions. The theory is that their owners solved the problem by simply releasing them into the wild. Other people responded more positively. Pam Mansfield opened the Exotic Pet Refuge at Deeping St James in the very south of Lincolnshire, and now has over 400 'refugees'.

One problem with this theory, though, is that sightings of big cats did not become common until the mid-1990s. Even then, some people had difficulty taking them seriously. On 28 September 1998 no less a person than Sir David Attenborough dismissed the whole business out of hand, but on the same day the local press reported another sighting at Covenham. The BBC's expert could not stem the rising tide of public interest, however, which was stimulated further by similar reports from across the whole of the country. In January 1999, after a sighting at Minting, the *Daily Mail* persuaded one of its intrepid reporters to venture out of London on a wild beast search, but sadly he found nothing.

Sceptics eagerly seized on the inevitable clutch of over-enthusiastic reports, which could be proved wrong. For instance the supposed paw prints of the Wolds panther found in a garden in Walesby during December 1998, were dismissed as those of a dog. A video of a big cat taken at Woodhall Spa was analysed by a zoo expert who said it was nothing more exciting than a large domestic cat.

Yet the fact that *some* of the reports have been cast into doubt does not mean that all the stories are untrue. There have been such a large number of sightings, by a wide range of people that it is impossible to avoid the conclusion that some form of big cats are out there. But until a lucky individual manages to get a good photograph, the mystery of exactly what type of cat – let alone how many – remains unsolved.

So, when walking the Lincolnshire fens, or when out driving, keep a watch for glistening, yellow eyes staring at you from out of the darkness. Dangerous wild animals have returned to Lincolnshire, the big cats are again at large.

WHEN LOVE TURNED SOUR

———————❁———————

Charles Dickens once wrote that 'a highly popular murder has been committed', by which he meant the sort of murder that people loved to read about. These cases were not the usual drunken brawl in a back street pub. Rather, they contained some added spice in the form of passion, rejected love, and at least a hint of the 'better' classes. Such murders were popular most of all with newspaper editors, because the details could fill columns of dense Victorian newsprint and sell plenty of copies.

In 1875, on 12th March, the *Lincolnshire Chronicle* flew off the presses with rather greater haste than usual, and was soon being read by one and all in the far-flung villages and hamlets of the county. In all the pubs, of town and country, working men settled down to enjoy a lively discussion about the ghastly details of a local murder.

'One of those heartless, cruel and deliberate crimes which startle and shock a community was perpetrated here on Saturday night,' announced the Louth correspondent of the *Chronicle* with almost too much enthusiasm to be decent. Murder was still quite rare in the county and this one had a few little extras, which made it genuinely different, including, above all, a beautiful and tragic victim of love turned sour. A young woman from a decent family was dead – and not just any young woman, but one of 'prepossessing appearance much esteemed by all who knew her'. The readers of Lincolnshire turned the pages and searched for the details. This is the story that enthralled them.

Peter Blanchard was a familiar sight around the Newmarket in Louth and along the street at the Free Methodist chapel. Blanchard, who was 26, had spent most of the last four years in pursuit of attractive Louisa Hodgson. The quietly prosperous Hodgson family lived in the middle of the town, where they were well-connected in the ironwork trade. Louisa was 22, an age at which she could be expected to marry, and Blanchard had expectations that they would eventually become husband and wife. They went to the chapel together every Sunday, even twice sometimes. In his mind, which was perhaps already troubled and turbulent, Louisa was already his betrothed and he hoped that the new year of 1875 would see his marriage to the young woman for whom he had waited so patiently.

But all went wrong for him. Blanchard was moody and difficult and the relationship with Louisa caused the Hodgson parents a great deal of worry. As 1874 drew to a close, the parents must have discussed their worries with Louisa. It seems she felt the same way for there is no evidence that she fought against the decision to end the unofficial engagement. Just before Christmas, they broke the news to Blanchard, who did not take it well and plunged ever more deeply into the dark moods which were troubling him.

Louth was a small country town, with a population of only a few thousand, so everybody knew everybody. The Hodgsons and Blanchard were also connected through their Free Methodist leanings and this brought about further complications. Blanchard had a brother, whose friend, John Campion, had carried a torch for Louisa for many a long month. He also went to the chapel, where he probably glanced furtively at the attractive young woman sitting with Blanchard and wondering whether life would ever deal him a similar opportunity.

When Blanchard was put on notice by the Hodgson parents, Campion saw his chance. He was a young and prosperous

Peter Blanchard and Louisa Hodgson attended this Free Methodist chapel in Eastgate, Louth

The idyllic country town of Louth was the setting for turbulent emotions and savage retribution

farmer with a good name and he already knew Louisa and must have sensed that his attentions were encouraged. Within weeks of the split with Blanchard, Louisa was 'keeping company' with Campion and this time all the old ladies of Louth said marriage was a certaintty.

Blanchard was torn apart by jealousy. He stopped going to the chapel, perhaps because he could not bear to see Louisa smiling at another man. He hung around in the streets nearby, however, when he might expect to see them. He probably hoped to catch her on her own, to plead for another chance. But Campion was firmly installed as a family favourite and was a regular guest at the Hodgson home in Newmarket.

One fateful Sunday afternoon, on the 7th March 1875, John Campion went for tea with the Hodgsons. He sat politely in the front parlour, talking pleasantly with the parents who were no doubt sizing up his potential as a son-in-law. But this was never to be. Louisa's nemesis was already skulking about in the evening shadows, waiting for another chance to argue his case. When Campion left the house with Louisa, heading off to the chapel as usual, Blanchard accosted the couple. He began trying to talk to Louisa, until Campion told him to leave her alone. He ignored the farmer, making such a nuisance of himself that Campion threatened to 'give him a good thrashing'. It made no difference, for Blanchard followed them up the street and only stopped annoying them at the chapel door.

The young couple went inside, while Blanchard slipped back to his lodgings to collect a knife and a cut-throat razor. The black clouds in his mind were gathering into a storm of anger and resentment.

When the chapel service finished, at about half past seven, Blanchard was again waiting outside. He accompanied the Hodgson family, and Campion, back to the house in Newmarket and strangely was allowed inside. Even more surprising, Louisa went into the front room with the turbulent Blanchard, while her parents, sister and Campion congregated in the kitchen at the back.

Why did they make the fateful decision to leave Louisa alone with Blanchard? It can only have been because she wished it. Perhaps she still had some lingering affection for him and wanted to ease his suffering by trying to explain once more that they could no longer be a couple. Perhaps she wanted to warn him that Campion really would sort him out if he carried on being a nuisance. No one can answer these questions, because she was not destined to survive the encounter.

The rest of the Hodgson family stayed in the kitchen, perhaps looking nervously at each other when they heard the sound of raised voices from the front room. It was clear that the discussion was not reaching any agreement, for both Louisa and Blanchard could be heard speaking forcefully. Nonetheless, no one left the kitchen to check, until at about ten o' clock there was sudden scuffle in the passageway that ran from the front room to the kitchen.

Then there was the scream of a woman.

Mrs Hodgson was first on her feet and as she opened the kitchen door Louisa fell through. 'He's stabbed me!' she shrieked. All was confusion for, with the voluminous clothes beloved of the Victorians, there was no sign of blood on Louisa.

'Where has he stabbed you?' her father asked as, slumping forwards, Louisa spoke her last words. 'In the heart,' she sobbed, and died almost instantly. A knife had pierced her lung and plunged into her heart.

Meanwhile, Blanchard had fled the scene of his crime. He turned into Vickers Lane and went to the home of his landlady's son, Turner. Pausing only to ask for and down a glass of whisky, he blurted out, 'I have done it. I have stabbed the Missus.' The words had a certain finality to them, as if he had been considering the act for a long time, but also reveal his distorted view of the situation in the way he identified his victim.

He stayed with Turner long enough to reveal more details. He explained that he had used a butcher's knife, but then drew a razor out of his pocket so that his friend could see he would have used that as well if necessary. It was enough of a confession to guarantee he would hang.

The alarm was sounded, and Sergeant Wilkinson of Louth police was soon on the scene. It must have been a momentous day for him, for murder was rare in country towns like this. Wilkinson quickly got hold of the basic details and organised a search, which soon turned up the butcher's knife 200 yards from the murder scene, in Aswell Lane. 'There is a stain like blood on the haft,' the policeman later told the coroner.

Soon Blanchard was in custody, but he made no attempt to hide his guilt. 'It is a good job; I am damned glad of it,' he said, before he realised that Louisa was actually dead. When told that she was, he retorted, 'Oh I did it and I'll die like a man for it.'

The trial was held at Lincoln in July 1875. By then, Blanchard had perhaps had time to reflect upon his defiant confessions and he began to consider any possibility for escaping the hangman's noose. He had confessed to Turner and the police, so there was no doubt of his guilt, but even in 1875 it was possible to escape the gallows if you could prove insanity. He perhaps got off to a good start when, asked how he pleaded, Blanchard simply replied, 'I don't know.'

Various witnesses were called to present a case that his life had been turned around by illness of the mind. It was said that he had been 'a bright and cheery lad' until an attack of typhoid fever in 1869. His friend, Turner, reported that he had seen Blanchard having fits, sometimes for up to three-quarters of an hour. Blanchard failed to lay a convincing trail whilst in gaol, however, because he had had no fits at all in the previous four months and had eaten so healthily that he had put on 25 pounds!

The jury was entirely unimpressed by the doubtful claims of insanity. They took only 15 minutes to reach the inevitable 'guilty' verdict but also entered a plea for mercy. The judge was unmoved and routinely put on the black cap and read out the death sentence, after which Blanchard himself was permitted to speak.

'I loved her so much,' he told the court, in the first words of what a cynic might have interpreted as the start of his campaign for clemency. 'I never believed I had killed her until I got one of her funeral cards, for I had never anything against her.' Whipping up the emotion, he then entered an appeal that must have distressed the dead girl's family. Blanchard asked that he could be buried beside his beloved Louisa. He then commenced on the traditional 'warnings against youthful folly' type of speech, offering the advice to 'Keep out of bad company.' He explained that his own slide to destruction had begun with smoking, then drinking and gambling, leading to the neglect of chapel. 'Look to Jesus,' he told the court, 'or some of you may be standing where I am next year.'

All this was in vain, for Blanchard was shown no mercy. The night before his execution, he sat down and wrote a letter to Campion, who he had been told was very distressed. Whether Campion was pleased to receive such a letter we do not know. The condemned man went to bed at midnight and rose at six, eating a small breakfast. Then he wrote a last farewell to his parents and at eight o' clock took the sacrament with the chaplain, before executioner Marwood arrived for the pinioning.

Public executions had been outlawed. Nonetheless, Blanchard's death was a melancholy scene. 'The loud pealing of thunder, the flashes of the lightning and the steady downpour of rain rendered the ceremony more than usually distressing,' wrote a local journalist in the *Lincolnshire Chronicle*.

Blanchard had totally abandoned his attempt to appear insane, but remained true to his renewed religious faith in his last moments. Just before nine he ascended the gallows steps and paused to speak to a small crowd of officials. 'I hope to meet you all in heaven, dear fellows,' he said. Then the bag was placed over his head, the noose tightened around his neck and the drop suddenly released. He fell five feet before the rope gripped tight with just the crown of his head visible to the watching few. But his neck did not break in the drop as it should have done. He lost consciousness gradually, taking fully two minutes to die, while the onlookers watched the jerking movements of his head. Then a black flag was eventually hoisted to tell the waiting public outside that the law had taken its course. Thus ended a tragic affair that destroyed two families and plunged a whole town into sorrow.

All that was left was for the executioner, Marwood, to pack his bags and slink quietly out of town, but word of the botched execution had spread. In the city of Lincoln, crowds hunted the streets looking for him on his way to the station. Two men were mistaken for Marwood and chased through the streets. Meanwhile the real man went into hiding for the rest of the day, before taking a cab to the Great Northern station the following morning. Even then, though, he was spotted by an angry crowd, who hissed and hooted at him. Some threatened violence, and the stationmaster had to lock him up in a secure office until his train arrived.

SCUNTHORPE'S INTERNATIONAL MAN OF MYSTERY

———————— ❁ ————————

The 1930s were a time of harsh reality, with low wages, high unemployment and few opportunities for the young to escape the supervision of their parents. The only fantasy world was provided by the picture houses, which brought a touch of glamour to every town and quite a few villages as well since there were even mobile cinemas to reach the most remote corners of the county. For those who could afford it, this glamorous other world was further brought to life through the pages of the glossy magazines.

The feeling of being trapped was worse for young women. Men, at least, could fly the nest and set off for the bright lights of London by themselves. For a young woman to do such a thing would have been regarded as a disgrace. Even education offered little respite for the average woman, when the most she could hope for was a job in the typing pool. So what every girl dreamed of was a handsome, sophisticated hero of her own (preferably with money) to sweep her off her feet. He could then take her to fashionable London restaurants, and launch her into a new life of exotic locations and romantic experience.

Irene Hinchliffe of Winteringham was one such young woman. She was described in one newspaper as 'only a country girl who was easily led,' and, at 24, Irene was already past the age when many of her friends were married with children of their own. Still living at home, she was desperate for a bit of excitement. Back Lane, Winteringham, made even Scunthorpe seem like some sort of exotic metropolitan paradise with its shops, dance halls, and eligible young men.

Irene lived in a small house with her mother, brother Arthur, and sometimes her father, who was often away driving a steam-roller for a living. Irene's mother sometimes went to join him and it was during one of these times away that Irene's life was turned upside down by the arrival of a mysterious, handsome and urbane young man. Irene and the young man wrote their own romance, which a newspaper later reported was 'the sort of story often read in books, but rarely met with in reality'.

Arthur Vamplew seemed to Irene like a real man of the world. Fashionably dressed, with an air of confidence and sophistication about him, he could talk expertly about both the London nightlife and foreign lands. He discussed the expensive flat he was buying in the West End, and hinted at lucrative business deals. As if revealing a dangerous national secret, he suggested the work he had done in the RAF was probably very secret and certainly very dangerous. He carried an air of mystery about him, and Irene was captivated by the hints of the exciting world, which the handsome Vamplew seemed to inhabit. So entranced was she that she did not pause to consider the biggest mystery of all. How did such a sophisticated charmer happen to be hanging around Scunthorpe and Winteringham with no obvious supply of cash?

Unfortunately for Vamplew, Mrs Hincliffe returned rather suddenly from one of her trips to Liverpool to visit her husband. Young, handsome and good with words, Arthur Vamplew cut no ice with the irate Mrs Hinchcliffe. She threw him out of the house before any explanation could be offered, quickly assessing the character of the mysterious stranger and deciding it was not up to much. But the Vamplew mystery turned out to be rather deeper and more complex than she imagined, and certainly more complicated than poor Irene believed.

Vamplew waited in the garden, where Irene soon joined him. No doubt the row that followed would not have been out of place in a modern day soap opera and was highly entertaining for the neighbours. Mrs Hinchliffe marched out and demanded from the young man an explanation as to who he was. When Irene started shouting back at her mother. 'We were married at Brigg Registry Office yesterday,' probably every curtain in the road twitched with the thrill of the scandal. This mysterious young man was Irene's new husband!

It probably took a few seconds for Mrs Hinchliffe to digest this startling revelation but she would not be beaten. Various scenarios raced through her mind. Her daughter had married a man she herself had never met so perhaps Irene was pregnant and this was an impulse wedding. She was able to compose herself, however, and demand, not unreasonably, 'Where's the marriage certificate?'

No doubt there was another pause whilst Irene and Arthur considered how best to answer this. It was Arthur who came up with a plausible excuse. He explained that, because he was in the Royal Air Force, he had had to post the certificate off to his base in order to get his married man's allowance. By degrees, Arthur was able to win his new 'mother-in-law' round, putting his knowledge of the RAF to good use. Mrs Hinchcliffe warmed to him, and allowed Arthur to lodge in her house with his bride. Arthur assured her that the RAF would send the certificate back.

As the days went by and no certificate arrived in the post, Mrs Hinchcliffe began to have new doubts about this young man who slept with her daughter, sat by her fire and ate her food. He didn't do any work and he hadn't produced any certificate. Indeed, his 'leave' from the RAF also seemed to be rather generous. Determined not to have the wool pulled over her eyes again, Mrs Hinchcliffe went off to the registry office in Brigg to check about the marriage. The staff at Brigg declared that her daughter's marriage was as much a mystery to them as Vamplew himself was to everybody.

Mrs Hinchcliffe returned to Winteringham in no mood for compromise. She launched straight into an attack on the deceiving Irene, who was no match for her mother in a rage. Instead she appealed to her mother's sense of decency. 'I may as well tell you we have not been married,' she said, 'The only way to right the wrong would be to get married decently now.' This was a cunning answer, for Mrs Hinchcliffe would know that the marriage of Irene and the mysterious Mr Vamplew was the only way to avoid the shame of a public scandel.

They went to Winteringham church to see the vicar about reading the banns. This would take three Sundays, then they could be married. Meanwhile, Vamplew confessed to another problem. His money from the RAF had not reached him yet and he was short of a bob or two. Mrs Hinchcliffe, reluctantly, agreed to help him out. She paid for the banns to be read, lent him some money for new shoes and even gave him cigarettes. It was agreed that he should pay a pound a week for his keep, but this would have to be paid in arrears. No doubt Mrs Hinchcliffe was suspicious, but she feared that if she put too much pressure on him he might run off and, for all she knew, Irene might already be pregnant.

The wedding was set for 7 October 1931, and the couple needed somewhere to live. Mrs Hinchcliffe found a cottage for them in the village and prepared for the wedding. The day before the ceremony was due to take place, Mrs Hinchcliffe returned to find the house empty. The young couple had gone. This was an unexpected turn of events. She could believe that Vamplew would run off, but never that they would *both* disappear before their wedding!

To start with, Irene's mother was helpless. All she could do was report the matter to the police. She then realised she could get her own back on the persuasive Vamplew. Hadn't she lent him money on the basis that he was marrying her daughter?

Hadn't she fed and clothed him, and given him an 'advance' on his wages? And now he had run off, no doubt as part of a plan not to pay her back. So she brought a charge against him. Arthur Vamplew became a wanted man for obtaining food, clothing, cigarettes and money under false pretences.

Mrs Hinchcliffe did not have long to wait. Two days after the elopement, she received a message to say that Irene had been found in London. The errant daughter was alone, penniless and hungry, without the means to get shelter or refreshment. Vamplew had disappeared, callously abandoning her amidst the bright lights she had so yearned to see. Chastened, she was brought back to Winteringham to face the wrath of her mother and the scorn of the village. She also had to give a full explanation.

Irene said that she had been introduced to Vamplew by his landlady. Reports said that he was from Messingham Road, Ashby, or alternatively from Smithfield Road. Vamplew had taken a fancy to Irene or, perhaps, saw in her a gullible and desperate woman who offered a chance of a bit of fun and maybe money. Whatever the reason, he turned up at the Hinchcliffe house while the mother was away and, according to Irene, would not leave. Irene said that he had more or less forced her and her brother into letting him stay for the night – though she declared he had slept with her brother Arthur. He stayed for several days, although on one occasion she had given him some money to get the bus back to his lodgings because he said he had left all his money there. He had not got on the bus, which was why he was still there when her mother returned. She had got into a panic about what Mrs Hinchcliffe would think, but Vamplew had given her a ring and told her to make up the registry office story. Later Irene had heard a rumour that Vamplew was already married, but he had denied it.

The people of Winteringham probably had many a conversation about the likely merits of Irene's story. Most of them probably came to the conclusion that she was being economical with the truth. Why would she have so enthusiastically defended the young man in front of her mother, if he was some unpleasant stray who had forced his way into their home? Why did she agree to marry him if there was nothing to be scandalised about? The old ladies of Winteringham could see plenty of reasons to doubt Irene's complete innocence in the whole affair.

Irene still had to explain the elopement to London, which, in the view of many, confirmed the rumour about Vamplew being already married. If he had gone through with the wedding at Winteringham church it would have been bigamy, a criminal offence, which carried a prison sentence. Vamplew had wisely fled, it seemed, but it was impossible to believe that Irene had gone along innocently.

It would seem that, a few days before the wedding, Vamplew came into some money. This was probably his RAF pay, but at least he had some cash in his pocket and this gave him renewed confidence and swagger. He began to describe to Irene the furnished flat that he had in London and the job that was waiting for him when he got there. Irene was so enthralled that she agreed to go with him to London where he promised he would marry her.

What happened in London we can only guess at, but when Vamplew came to court the 'prosecution agreed to withhold certain details'. Irene's expectations of romance and passionate abandonment had been dashed. Having been told that she would be staying at the Imperial Hotel until Vamplew's flat was ready, she ended up sleeping on Paddington station.

Irene returned to her mother's clutches, but the mysterious Vamplew managed to disappear for a few weeks. At the end of November, however, he was arrested and brought back to Scunthorpe to face charges and an angry wife, who promptly sued for divorce. The international playboy, full of charm and sophistication, was brought to book by a clutch of vengeful women. Vamplew himself came to court in December 1931 on the charges of obtaining goods and money worth £6-15s from Mrs Hinchcliffe by deception. Irene's shame was dragged through the newspapers and her mysterious, exotic lover turned out to be a cheap charlatan.

Vamplew pleaded not guilty, but the evidence of his despicable conduct was so overwhelming that his counsel interrupted the proceedings to tell him to change his plea to guilty or counsel would cease to represent him. Vamplew agreed to do this, and thus spared Irene from a humiliating cross-examination. He was sent to prison for three months, whilst Irene returned to a quiet life in Winteringham.

THE STICKNEY MURDERESS

———————❖———————

Priscilla Biggadyke, known as 'the Stickney Murderess' was sentenced to death in 1868 for a murder which she maintained she did not commit. The jury even admitted, when delivering the guilty verdict, that the evidence was purely circumstantial. Nonetheless, Priscilla Biggadyke went to the scaffold, on 28th December 1868, protesting her innocence to the end. She died painfully, due to the incompetence of the hangman. It was a grizzly end to a miserable life.

Priscilla Whiley was born in 1833 at Gedney. She married Richard Biggadyke in 1855 and they lived in a one-bedroom cottage at Stickney. They were on the bottom rung of Lincolnshire society. Neither of them could read or write and they had no prospects. Biggadyke himself was variously described as a 'farmhand' and 'wellsinker'. To alleviate their poverty the couple had to take in lodgers. They only had two rooms and they already had two children, so lodgers and family all slept in the same room. A third child was born in 1868.

The lodgers could not have been more different. George Ironmonger was a young fisherman, described as being of 'a smart appearance' and about 21 years old. Thomas Proctor was a rat catcher who kept ferrets and by all accounts was a very unsavoury looking character. In one report he is described as being 'the most uncouth-looking individual in the whole parish, his countenance is very repugnant. He has a high back and his legs appear to have a serious malformation.'

Unfortunately, it was the lodgers, more specifically Proctor, that caused a rift between the Biggadykes. Richard began to suspect that the relationship between his 'good-looking' wife and the lodgers was more than just a commercial one. In fact he became convinced that when he was out at work Priscilla and Proctor were 'laying together' and that the third child was not his own. According to the *Chronicle*, the overcrowded living conditions in the cottage were such that 'immorality was invited' and led to an atmosphere of hatred and distrust between the Biggadykes.

When Richard expressed doubts about the baby being his, his wife did not exactly allay his fears by replying, 'Well, it is mine at any rates.' On another occasion when Priscilla was seen in a new dress, her neighbour remarked that Richard must have come into some money but Mrs Biggadyke remarked that 'it was not bought with HIS money'.

The village of Stickney was already rife with rumours about Priscilla and Proctor, and some reports that Ironmonger was also her lover. The sudden death of Richard Biggadyke provided powerful fuel for the boilers of rumour, which were soon overheating.

That fateful day came on 30th September 1868, when Richard Biggadyke returned home from work at about 6 pm. He ate his supper of mutton, shortcake and tea and within a few minutes he became violently ill. He started 'retching and purging' in dramatic fashion. Doctor Maxwell was sent for and found that Biggadyke had 'extreme inflammation of the stomach' but could do little to help the distressed man. He prescribed some medication but after hours of pain and torment, Biggadyke died at six o' clock the next morning.

Subsequently, many neighbours and gossipmongers came forward to say that they had heard Priscilla say things about her husband such as, 'I'd like to see him brought home dead.' During the course of the inquest, carried out by the coroner, W Clegg, these reports indicated a possible motive for murder. It was increasingly clear that Mrs Biggadyke and possibly Thomas Proctor were in serious difficulties.

The real evidence, though, concentrated on the evening meal and the administering of poison. Mrs Biggadyke had made three shortcakes for the evening meal and two of these had been eaten by the lodgers when they came home at 5 pm. The other was eaten by Biggadyke an hour later and was found to contain traces of arsenic. As a result, a charge of wilful murder was brought against Priscilla Biggadyke and Thomas Proctor.

Priscilla was arrested by Superintendent Wright on 3rd October. On the way to gaol she began talking about the situation, and said 'It is hard work I should bear all the blame, I am innocent.' She also told him that she had seen a note in her husband's pocket which said he had taken the poison himself due to his troubles, mainly debt. When Wright pointed out to her that Biggadyke had not been able to write, she said someone else must have written it for him. She also added that unfortunately she had burnt the note.

Mrs Biggadyke and Proctor were taken to Spilsby House of Correction. On 15th October, the former made a statement to the governor laying all the blame at the feet of Proctor. She stated that she had seen Proctor pour some white powder into her husband's tea cup and later into the medicine provided by the doctor. She had given this to him, but had also tasted a little for herself and claimed to have been sick for two days. Proctor steadfastly maintained his innocence, pronouncing, 'Well gentlemen, I shall be innocent, take me where you like', when sent for trial.

By the time of the trial, Priscilla Biggadyke had clearly turned against Proctor and was reported as 'cold' towards him throughout. Her appearance in the dock provoked mixed reactions among watching journalists. The *Chronicle* described her thus: 'The prisoner would be considered a good looking woman but for the smallness of her eyes, which gave an impression of great determination. She is thickset, about five feet two inches. She was meanly attired and her straw bonnet was very dirty, and had evidently seen much service.'

The combination of sex and poverty seems to have aroused the enthusiasm of the national press. The *Guardian* wrote that the case 'revealed a depth of moral depravity and social degradation we could fair hope has no parallel in the county of Lincoln'.

During the trial the evidence piled up but none of it was concrete. Mrs Ironmonger, the grandmother of one of the Biggadyke's lodgers, put the finger of blame firmly in Priscilla's direction by testifying that the accused had had some white powder for killing mice some months earlier. There was never any dispute about the fact that it was Priscilla who had made the tea which killed her husband, even though it could not be proved when the poison was added or by whom.

There was also much discussion about Priscilla's insistence that Proctor was the murderer. She confirmed that he had been there when her husband was eating. Her theory was a little confused, however. Although she stuck to her story that Proctor had put white powder into both Mr Biggadyke's tea, and into his medicine, she had also raised the question that it may have been suicide, because of the mysterious note she had mentioned.

Samples of Biggadyke's vomit had been preserved by the doctor and some of his organs had been sent to a Professor Taylor, for analysis. The professor testified with certainty that the deceased had been killed with arsenic, stating categorically, 'I never saw a clearer case of death by poison.' No poison, however, was found in the house, perhaps because the search was carried out three days after the murder!

The motive seemed to be clear, a disgruntled wife, fed up with her lot. And there were plenty of witnesses willing to testify that Biggadyke himself had blamed his wife for his state in his last hours. According to one, he had thrown a cup at her and knocked her backwards.

In the judge's summing up, he drew particular attention to the different stories told by Priscilla Biggadyke, that it was suicide or that Proctor was to blame. In the event, the jury reached a verdict of 'guilty' without even leaving the box, but asked the judge for mercy because the evidence was based on supposition. The judge was unmoved and donned the customary black cap to pronounce the sentence of death by hanging.

As the bells of Lincoln rang out the joyous news of Christmas they brought no glad tidings of hope for the condemned woman, whose execution date had been set for 28th December.

During the days in the run up to her execution, Priscilla was visited many times by the chaplain. No matter what he said to her, she refused to make any confession of guilt, thus condemning her soul to eternal damnation. She also had a letter dictated to the employers of George Ironmonger, the details of which soon got into the papers. Biggadyke asked Ironmonger to seek forgiveness of his sins, to 'mourn her sad end', and pleaded with him to look after her children who would soon become orphans.

Young Ironmonger, clearly stirred by the letter, presented himself at the Castle gates, where she was being held, two days before sentence was due to be carried out. Unfortunately he was refused permission to speak to his former landlady and turned away unable to offer any words of comfort. The same day, though, her brother and three sisters were allowed to visit for a short while. It was a turbulent meeting, during which the siblings struggled to win over their sister's soul by encouraging her to confess her guilt. As they put more and more pressure on her, Priscilla apparently flew into a rage of 'passionate excitement' inspired by a black despair and anger at her fate. The family interview came to an unhappy end and they left without having secured the confession.

In her last two days, Priscilla sank into abject despair. She had been denied a sight of her older children although her baby had been with her for a time. Priscilla's thoughts now turned to suicide, but her attempts to get hold of the means were thwarted by vigilant gaolers. First a garter, and then a handkerchief, were confiscated. On her last night she even pleaded with a woman gaoler to change clothes with her so that she might escape, a request which was ignored not surprisingly.

On the day of her execution the prison chaplain, Reverend Richter, made one more attempt to hear her confession. But to no avail.

The gallows or 'drop' had been erected just east of the Crown Court building, about two hundred yards from the prison door. Nowadays it is a pleasant grassy area where tourists linger and children play. As Priscilla was escorted along the last few yards of her life's journey, she finally gave up all care of living, saying 'I hope my troubles are ended'. She was then placed on a chair, in full view of the scaffold, while Richter preached the condemned sermon.

'I had hoped that you would have made that confession,' he argued, 'and thus have enabled me, as a minister of Christ, to have pronounced the forgiveness of your sins, under the promise that Christ came into this world to save sinners. It has grieved me very much to find that you still persist in the declaration that you are not accountable for your husband's death; that you still say that you did not administer the poison yourself, that you did not see any other person administer it, and that you are entirely free of the crime. Do you say so now?'

Firmly, and with certainty, Biggadyke replied. 'Yes.'

With this, Richter seems to have abandoned the task, exclaiming, 'I must leave you to God.'

The condemned woman then spoke her final words, 'All my troubles are over. Shame, you're going to hang me. Surely my troubles are over', as the cathedral bells tolled the hour. The executioner, Thomas Askern then drew the bolt and watched Priscilla Biggadyke drop. Unfortunately the noose had been incorrectly positioned and it took several minutes for Priscilla to die.

Priscilla was buried in the bleak interior of the old Lucy Tower, where it is still possible to see her gravestone. It is a simple slab carved with her initials P.B., and Dec. 28, 1868 underneath.

This sad story did not end with the execution of Priscilla Biggadyke. The baby, of unproven origins, was taken to the workhouse where it died two years later. Thomas Proctor married and began his own family, existing as a 'rag and bone dealer' in Stickney. But in early 1882 he too became ill, though this time of natural causes, and began to prepare for his own journey into eternity. Faced with the prospect of eternal damnation he at last unburdened his own soul by telling what he knew. He confessed that he had indeed put the poison in the tea and then stood by to watch an innocent woman die in his place.

His deathbed confession was apparently reported in the *Daily Telegraph* and led to a pardon for the unfortunate Priscilla, a victim of the irrevocable system of capital punishment.

The grave of Priscilla Bigggadyke at Lincoln Castle is surrounded by those of convicted murderers and thieves